clas.
. variet
of basic
- ways of
  munities a
- techniques
  riculum mat
  ing materia
- classroom
  discipline
- the social a
  schools
- methods of
  strategies fo
  flict
- criticism ar

Practical
TEACHING is
setting out to te
taught for a whi.
ing."

SCHOCKEN B(
200 Madison A
New York City

ISBN 0-805
Jacket design by

On Teaching

HERBERT R. KOHL

SCHOCKEN BOOKS • NEW YORK

First published by SCHOCKEN BOOKS 1976

Copyright © 1976 by Herbert R. Kohl

Library of Congress Cataloging in Publication Data

Kohl, Herbert R.
  On teaching.

  Bibliography: p. 179
  Includes index.
  1. Teaching. I. Title.

LB1025.2.K62   371.1'02   76-9131

Manufactured in the United States of America

*To Aunt Addie Gallardo, who first
showed me the importance of letters*

CONTENTS

PREFACE

THIS BOOK IS for people thinking about becoming a teacher as well as for people in teacher training and for people who are in the classroom and think of themselves as still learning how to teach. It is about the specifics of working with children and developing curriculum material. It is also about educational politics, the social structure of the school, and the ways in which the feelings we have as adults affect the work we do in school. It is a putting together of things I have seen and thought about and tried over the past fifteen years in regular public schools and alternative schools, with children from kindergarten through senior high school. I hope this book will provide useful information and be able to serve as a handbook for the practicing teacher, something that fits in the box of tools and tricks and poster board and magic markers and reference books that we rely on as we try to fit our work to the needs of the students we work with.

I would like to thank all the teachers who have taught me, all of the people I have worked with at the Center for Open Learning and Teaching, and of course all the young people I have worked with. Special thanks are due Marcie McGaugh, my typist, who never lets a silly word or foolish statement go, and the editors I have worked with at *Teacher* magazine for whom some of the material in this book was originally prepared.

On Teaching

1. *INTRODUCTION*

IT TAKES YEARS to learn how to teach well, and even then one never learns once and for all. Teaching is not like driving a car or adding a column of figures. Each group of students one works with has different needs and presents new challenges. Like any craft, one learns teaching by practicing it and by finding models, other teachers whose practice one admires and can study.

Teacher training programs provide just a beginning. There is a limit to what one can learn in a seminar room or student teaching in someone else's class. The essentials of learning to teach begin when one has the responsibility for a class or a group of young people. At that point it begins to be possible to know what resources are needed, what knowledge is useful, what questions need to be answered by more experienced teachers, and what skills one needs. This short book is for people setting out to teach and for people who have taught for a while and feel they are still learning.

I've been teaching for most of the past fifteen years and have worked in all the grades except for the third and fourth, in traditional public schools where I felt uncomfortable and under enormous pressure, and in alternative public schools where we could do pretty much what we wanted but also experienced political pressure. Learning to teach well has been one of the themes of my life. Another has been learning to survive while doing it.

Survival, the ability to acquire and use political power for humane purposes, and the development of the craft of teaching are the themes of this book. It is possible to close the door of one's classroom and concentrate exclusively on work with one's students. It is also possible to become obsessed with politics and forget that teaching well involves more than having decent ideas and struggling for justice. The tension between politics and good practice as a teacher has to be accepted and integrated into one's life. Teaching is serious, difficult work. It has to do with the future, with whom we encourage our young people to be, and ultimately, of course, with who we will be as a nation and as people sharing the earth. It is not simply a job, especially if you question the system you work and live in and set out to change it. It involves risks, enormous humor and good feeling, play, conflict, and hard knowledge about things like reading and history and science and mathematics. Choosing to become a teacher is not a light decision.

A while ago I was involved in a teacher training program for the Center for Open Learning and Teaching and the University Without Walls, Berkeley. In planning our program we found ten crucial issues that student teachers and beginning teachers must attend to. On re-reading them, it became clear that all of us who are serious about our work with young people have to continually keep these issues in mind.

We all have to be able to:

1. clarify our motives for becoming teachers;
2. develop skills and competencies of our own besides those specifically involved in teaching;
3. learn a variety of approaches to the teaching of basic reading and mathematical skills;
4. get experience in understanding unfamiliar communities and cultures, preferably learning from peers from these communities;
5. practice developing curriculum to meet specific needs of particular children and communities;
6. learn how to modify existing material;
7. be able to organize a classroom and structure time with students as well as deal with verbal and physical conflict without resorting to oppression;
8. understand the social structure and politics of the schools;
9. have an awareness of techniques for organizing communities and dealing with political conflict; and
10. learn to accept criticism and be self-critical.

It takes experience, including defeat, failure, and frustration, to develop most of the skills mentioned above. It takes years to become established in a new community and then more time to develop an organization strong enough to fight oppressive schools effectively. With the best will in the world, it also takes years to learn to build the right tone in a class, and equip the room sensibly, to develop an eye for children in trouble, to know how to support students and how to make demands on them without oppressing them, to know when to add something new or step back and leave the children alone. Teaching is no simple matter. It is hard work, part craft, part art, part technique, part politics, and it takes time to develop ease within such a complex role. However, for many of us the effort makes sense, for one gets the opportunity to see young people grow while one has a positive and caring role in their lives.

The ways of dealing with this complex role of being a teacher committed to social and educational change that I've learned or heard of over the past fifteen years form the subject matter of this book.

2. WHY TEACH?

THERE ARE MANY reasons that lead people to choose elementary and secondary school teaching. Some people choose teaching because they enjoy being with young people and watching them grow. Others need to be around young people and let their students grow for them. Teaching for some is a family tradition, a craft that one naturally masters and a world that surrounds one from childhood. For others teaching is magical because they have had magical teachers whose roles they want to assume. Teaching can be a way of sharing power, of convincing people to value what you value, or to explore the world with you or through you.

There are some cynical reasons for going into teaching which were much more prevalent when getting a job was not difficult. For example, for some people teaching becomes a matter of temporary convenience, of taking a job which seems respectable and not too demanding while going to law school, supporting a spouse through professional or graduate school, scouting around for a good business connection, or merely marking time while figuring out what one really wants to do as an adult. For others teaching is a jumping-off point into administration, research, or supervision.

Many student teachers I have known over the last five years are becoming teachers to negate the wounds they received when they were in school. They want to counter the racism, the sexual put-downs, all the other humiliations they experienced with new, freer ways of teaching and learning. They want to be teachers to protect and nurture people younger than they who have every likelihood of being damaged by the schools. Some of these people come from poor or oppressed communities, and their commitment to the children is a commitment to the community of their parents, brothers and sisters, and their own children as well. Others, mostly from white middle- or upper-class backgrounds, have given up dialogue with their parents and rejected the community they grew up in. Teaching for them becomes a means of searching for ways of connecting with a community they can care for and serve.

There were a number of reasons that led me to choose elementary school teaching. For one, I never wanted to put my toys away and get on with the serious business of being an adult. I enjoy playing games, building things that have no particular purpose or value beyond themselves, trying painting, sculpting, macramé without becoming obsessed by them. I enjoy moving from subject to subject, from a math problem to a design problem, from bead collecting to the classification of mollusks. Specialization does not interest me, and teaching elementary school makes it possible for me to explore many facets of the world and share what I learn. My self-justification is that the games I play and the things I explore all contribute to making a curriculum that will interest and engage my students.

I guess also I became a teacher of young children initially because I thought they were purer, more open, and less damaged than I was. They were the saviors—they could dare to be creative where I was inhibited; they could write well because they didn't know what good writing was supposed to be; they could learn with ease, whereas I was overridden with anxiety over grades and tests. I never forgot the time in high school when I was informed that I missed making Arista, the national high school honor society, by 0.1 of a point. I went into the boys' bathroom and cried, the first time I had cried since being a baby. Neither Hitler's horrors nor the deaths of relatives and friends could cause me to cry because I was a male and was too proud to show sadness and weakness. Yet 0.1 of a grade point could bring tears and self-hatred and feelings of inferiority. And what if I'd made it—would I laugh at my friends' tears because they missed by 0.1 of a point just as they did at me? There is no reward on either side of that cruel system.

When I became a teacher, some of my dreams of free development for my own students came true—they could be open and creative. But they also could be closed, destructive, nasty, manipulating—all the things I wanted to avoid in the adult world. It was important to sort out the romance of teaching from the realities of teaching and discover whether, knowing the problems, the hard work and frustration, it still made sense to teach. For me the answer has been "yes," but there are still times I wish I'd chosen some easier vocation.

Everyone who goes into teaching, even temporarily, has many reasons for choosing to spend five hours a day with young people. These reasons are often unarticulated and more complex than one imagines. Yet they have significant effects upon everyday work with students and on the satisfaction and strength the teacher gets from that work. Consequently, it makes sense, if you are thinking of becoming a teacher, to begin questioning yourself and understanding what you expect from teaching and what you are willing to give to it.

It also is of value to understand what type of children, what age, what setting is most sensible for your temperament and skills. Simple mistakes like teaching children that are too young or too old can destroy promising teachers. I had a friend who was teaching first grade and having a miserable time of it. The class was out of order, the students paid no attention to what she said, and she couldn't understand what the children were talking about. One day in anger, she blurted out to me that her major frustration was that she couldn't hold a good conversation with her class. She wanted to talk about civil rights, racism, about ways of reconstructing our society, about poverty and oppression. She wanted to read poetry with the children, expose them to music. She prepared each class for hours, put herself into the work, cared about the children—and yet things kept on getting worse. What she wanted and needed from her six-year-olds was simply beyond them. I suggested that she try junior high if she wanted dialogue and challenge from her students. First grade was a mistake. The next year she transferred to one of the most difficult junior high schools in New York City, where she immediately felt at home. She was in the right place—what she offered could be used by the students, and therefore they could reward her with the exchange she needed.

There are a number of questions people thinking of becoming teachers might ask themselves in order to clarify their motives and focus on the type of teaching situations that could make sense for them. These questions do not have simple answers. Sometimes they cannot be answered until one has taught for a while. But I think it makes sense to keep them in mind while considering whether you actually want to teach and then, if you do, during training and the first few years of work.

1. What reasons do you give yourself for wanting to teach? Are they all negative (e.g., because the schools are oppressive, or because I was damaged, or because I need a job and working as a teacher is more respectable than working as a cab driver or salesperson)? What are the positive reasons for wanting to teach? Is there any pleasure to be gained from teaching? Knowledge? Power? As an elaboration on this, there is another similar question:

2. Why do you want to spend so much time with young people? Are you afraid of adults? Intimidated by adult company? Fed up with the competition and coldness of business and the university? Do you feel more comfortable with children? Have you spent much time with children recently, or are you mostly fantasizing how they would behave? Before deciding to become a teacher, it makes sense to spend time with young people of different ages at camp, as a tutor, or as a playground supervisor. I have found it valuable to spend time at playgrounds and observe children playing with each other or relating to their parents or teachers. One day watch five-, ten-, fifteen-year-olds on the playground or the street, and try to see how they are alike and how they are different. The more you train your eye to observe young people's behavior, the easier it will be to pick up attitudes and feelings and relationships in your own classroom.

Elaborating on the question of why spend so much time with young people, it is important to ask . . .

3. What do you want from the children? Do you want them to do well on tests? Learn particular subject matter? Like each other? Like you? How much do you need to have students like you? Are you afraid to criticize them or set limits on their behavior because they might be angry with you? Do you consider yourself one of the kids? Is there any difference in your mind between your role and that of your prospective students?

Many young teachers are not sure of themselves as adults, feel very much like children and cover over a sense of their own powerlessness with the rhetoric of equality. They tell their students that they are all equal and then are surprised when their students walk all over them or show them no respect. If students have to go to school, if the teacher is paid and the students are not, if the young expect to learn something from the older in order to become more powerful themselves, then the teacher who pretends to be an equal of the student is both a hypocrite and a disappointment in the students' eyes. This does not mean that the teacher doesn't learn with or from the students, nor does it mean that the teacher must try to coerce the students into learning or be the source of all authority. It does mean, however, that the teacher ought to have some knowledge or skills to share, mastery of a subject that the students haven't already encountered and might be interested in. This leads to the next question:

4. What do you know that you can teach to or share with your students? Too many young people coming out of college believe that they do not know anything worth sharing or at least feel they haven't learned anything in school worth it. Teacher training usually doesn't help since it concentrates on "teaching skills" rather than the content of what might be learned. Yet there is so much young people will respond to if the material emerges out of problems that challenge them and if the solutions can be developed without constant judging and testing. I have found that young people enjoy working hard, pushing and challenging themselves. What they hate is having their self-esteem tied up in learning and regurgitating material that bores them. Constant testing interferes with learning.

The more you know, the easier teaching becomes. A skilled teacher uses all his or her knowledge and experience in the service of building a curriculum each year for the particular individuals that are in the class. If you cannot think of any particular skills you have, but just like being with children, don't go right into teaching. Find other ways of spending time with young people while you master some skills that you believe are worth sharing.

Here is a partial list of things one could learn: printing; working with wood, plastic, fabrics, metal; how to run a store; making or repairing cars, shoes, boats, airplanes; playing and teaching cards, board, dice, ball games; playing and composing music; understanding ways of calculating and the use and construction of computers; using closed circuit TV; making films;

taking pictures; understanding history, especially history that explains part of the present; knowing about animals and plants, understanding something of the chemistry of life; knowing the law; understanding how to use or care for one's body.

These subjects are intrinsically interesting to many students and can be used as well in teaching the so-called basic skills of reading, writing, and math, which are themselves no more than tools that extend people's power and make some aspects of the world more accessible. Too often these basic skills are taught in isolation from interesting content, leaving students wondering what use phonics or set theory could possibly have in their lives. It is not good enough to tell the class that what they are learning now will be of use when they are grown-ups. Six-year-olds and ten-year-olds have immediate interests, and reading and math ought to be tied to these interests, which range all the way from learning to make and build things to learning to play games and master comic books and fix bicycles and make money and cook and find out about other people's feelings and lives—the list can go on and on. The more time you spend informally with young children, the more you will learn about their interests. Listening carefully and following up on what you hear are skills a teacher has to cultivate. If students are interested in paper airplanes, it is more sensible to build a unit around flying than to ban them and assume police functions.

5. Getting more specific, a prospective teacher ought to consider what age youngster he or she feels greatest affinity toward or most comfortable with. There are some adults who are afraid of high school- or junior high school-aged people (thirteen- to seventeen-year-olds), while others are terrified at the idea of being left alone in a room with twenty-four six-year-olds. Fear of young people is neither unnatural nor uncommon in our culture. This is especially true in the schools, where undeclared warfare between the adults and the children defines much of the social climate. As long as young people feel constantly tested and judged by their teacher and have to experience the humiliation of their own or their friends' failures, they try to get even in any ways they can. Teachers who try to be kind often find themselves taken advantage of, while those who assume a strict stand are constantly tricked and mocked. It takes time and experience to win the respect of young people and

not be considered their enemy in the context of a traditional American school.

It is very difficult to feel at ease in a classroom, to spend five hours with young people, and not emerge wiped out or exhausted at the end of the day. This is especially true if one is mismatched with the students.

Great patience and humor, an ease with physical contact, and an ability to work with one's hands as well as one's mouth are needed for teachers of five- and six-year-olds. A lack of sexual prudery is almost a prerequisite for junior high school teachers, while physical and personal confidence and the love of some subject make work with high school students much easier.

This does not mean that an adult shouldn't take chances working with students whose age poses a problem. I know this year has been one of the most fulfilling of my teaching years, and yet I was full of anxiety about my ability to be effective with five- and six-year-olds after working with twelve- to eighteen-year-olds for twelve years. I taught myself to be patient, learned to work with my hands, to play a lot, to expect change to develop slowly. The students' ability to express affection or dislike openly and physically moved and surprised me, and initially their energy exhausted me. I must have lost fifteen pounds the first month, just trying to keep up with them.

One way of discovering what age youngster to begin working with is to visit a lot of schools. Try to find teachers you like and respect, and spend a few days working alongside them. Don't visit for an hour or two. It is important to stay all day (or if you have time, all week) to get a sense of the flow of time and energy working with that age person involves. Of course, your rhythm as a teacher might be different, but it is important to have a sense of what it is like to be with young people all day before becoming a teacher.

6. Before becoming a teacher it is important to examine one's attitudes toward racial and class differences. Racism is part of the heritage of white Americans, and though it can be mostly unlearned, it manifests itself in many subtle ways. Some white teachers are overtly condescending toward black and brown and red children, give them crayons instead of books. Others are more

subtly condescending—they congratulate themselves on caring enough to work in a ghetto, choose one or two favorite students and put the rest down as products of a bad environment. They consider themselves liberal, nonracist, and yet are repelled by most of their students while believing that they are "saving" a few. There are ways of picking up racist attitudes in one's own way of talking. When a teacher talks about his or her pupils as "them" or "these kind of children," or when a favorite pupil is described as "not like the rest of them," one is in the presence of a racist attitude. Accompanying this attitude is usually an unarticulated fear of the children. I have seen white kindergarten teachers treat poor black five-year-old boys as if they were nineteen, carried guns and knives, and had criminal intentions at all times. Needless to say, this sort of adult attitude confuses and profoundly upsets the child. It also causes the adult to ignore acts that should otherwise be prevented. Many white teachers in ghetto schools claim they are being permissive and believe in allowing their students freedom when it would be closer to the truth to say that they are afraid that their students will beat them up and that they are afraid to face the moral rage their students have from being treated in brutal and racist ways. When a student destroys a typewriter or brutalizes a smaller student, that is not an acceptable or humane use of freedom.

Young teachers have a hard time knowing how and when to be firm and when to be giving. This becomes even more complex when the teacher is white, of liberal persuasion, afraid of physical violence, and teaching a class of poor children who are not white.

However, fear is not limited to white-nonwhite situations. Many middle-class people have attitudes toward poor people in general that are manifested in the classroom in ways very close to the racist attitudes described above. Poverty is looked upon as a disease that one does not want to have contact with. Many teachers have a hard time touching poor children, as if somehow the poverty can be spread by physical contact. Then there are the condescending liberal attitudes toward "saving" a few good students from the general condition of poverty, as if the rest got what they deserve.

Prospective teachers, especially those who might choose or be assigned to work with poor or nonwhite students have to examine their own attitudes toward class and race. If these people come from isolated white middle-class communities, I would suggest they move into a mixed urban community and live and work there before becoming teachers. Then they might be able to see their students as individuals rather than as representatives of a class or race. And they might also develop insight into the different ways people learn and teach each other and themselves. Good teaching requires an understanding and respect of the strengths of one's pupils, and this cannot develop if they and their parents are alien to one's nonschool experience.

7. Another, perhaps uncomfortable, question a prospective teacher ought to ask him or herself is what sex-based motives he or she has for wanting to work with young people. Do you want to enable young boys or girls to become the boys or girls you could never be? To, for example, free the girls of the image of prettiness and quietness and encourage them to run and fight, and on an academic level, mess about with science and get lost in the abstractions of math? Or to encourage boys to write poetry, play with dolls, let their fantasies come out, and not feel abnormal if they enjoy reading or acting or listening to music?

Dealing with sex is one of the most difficult things teachers who care to have all their students develop fully have to learn how to manage. Often children arrive at school as early as kindergarten with clear ideas of what is proper behavior for boys and girls. The teacher has to be sensitive to parentally and culturally enforced sex roles that schools traditionally enforce, and be able to lead children to choose what they want to learn, free of those encumbrances

There are other problems teachers have to sort out that are sexual rather than sex-based. Many male teachers enjoy flirting with female students and using flirtation as a means of controlling the girls. Similarly, some female teachers try to seduce male students into learning. All these exchanges are covert—a gesture, a look, a petulant or joking remark.

Children take adult affection very seriously, and often what is play or dalliance on the part of the adult becomes the basis of endless fantasy and expectation on the part of the child. The issue exists in the early grades, but is much more overt on the high school level, where young teachers often naively express affection and concern, which students interpret as sexual overtures (which in some cases they might actually be, however unclear to the teacher).

Entering into an open relationship with a student is another issue altogether. Obviously, love is not bound to age or status. One should be wary, however, of confusing love with conquest and manipulation—but these problems are not limited to one's life as a teacher.

A final question that should be asked with respect to sex in the classroom: do you need to get even with one sex, as a group, for real or fancied injuries you experienced? Do you dislike boys or girls as a group? Do you feel that the girls were always loved too much? That the boys brutalized you and need to learn a lesson? That somehow you have to get even in your classroom for an injury you suffered as a child? There are many good reasons for not becoming a teacher, and the need to punish others for a hurt you suffered is certainly one.

It might seem that I'm being harsh or cynical by raising questions about motives for teaching and suggesting that there are circumstances in which a person either should not become a teacher or should wait a while. If anything, these questions are too easy and can unfortunately be put aside with facile, self-deceiving answers. But teaching young people—i.e., helping them become sane, powerful, self-respecting, and loving adults—is a very serious and difficult job in a culture as oppressive and confused as ours, and needs strong and self-critical people.

There are other questions that ought to be considered. These might seem less charged, but are not less important.

8. What kind of young people do you want to work with? There are a number of children with special needs that can be assisted by adults with particular qualities. For example, there are some severely disturbed children—children whose behavior is bizarre, who are not verbal, who might not yet be toilet-trained at nine or ten, who might be engaged in dialogue for hours at a time with creatures you cannot perceive. My first experience was at a school for severely disturbed children very much like those described above. I liked the children, but lasted only six months since I didn't have the patience. I needed them to recognize and engage me, even

through defiance. I couldn't bear their silence or removal, their unrelieved pain. As soon as I changed schools and began to work with normal, though angry and defiant, young people, I felt at home.

My wife, Judy, is different. She has the patience to live with small increments of change, is calm and gentle and nonthreatening to remote and scared children. She feels much more at home in silent or remote worlds than I do, and is an excellent teacher of disturbed children. It is a matter of knowing who you are and what the children need.

These same questions should be raised by people thinking of working with deaf, blind, or physically damaged people. Who are they? What is the world they live in? How can I serve them?

Let me illustrate a perverse way of going about deciding how to serve people in order to point toward a more healthy way of functioning. For a long time most schools for deaf children were controlled by nondeaf teachers, parents, and administrators who advocated the oral, rather than the manual, tradition. The oral tradition maintained that it was necessary for deaf individuals to learn to speak instead of depending on sign language. Many oralist schools prohibited their students from using sign language, and some professionals within that tradition maintained that sign language was not a "real" language at all, but some degenerate or primitive form of communication. All these prohibitions were to no avail—deaf children learned signing from each other and used it when the teachers' backs were turned. Many deaf adults trained in oralist schools ended up despising the language they were forced to learn and retreated into an all-deaf world where communication was in signs. Recently things have begun to change—sign language has been shown to be an expressive, sophisticated language with perhaps even greater potential for communication than oral language. A deaf-power movement has developed which insists that teachers of the deaf respond to the needs of deaf adults and children. It is no longer possible to tell deaf people what they must learn from outside the community. To teach within a deaf community (and, in fact, in all communities) requires understanding the world people live in and responding to their needs as they articulate them. This does not mean that the teacher should be morally or politically neutral. Rather, it means that being a teacher does not put an individual in a position of forcing his or her values on students or community. A teacher must engage in dialogue with the students and parents if he or she hopes to change them—and be open to change as well. Many teachers have been educated in communities they initially thought they would educate.

9. Some people get along well in crowds and others function best with small groups or single individuals. Before becoming a classroom teacher, it is important to ask oneself what the effect is on one's personality of spending a lot of time with over twenty people in the same room. Some of the best teachers I know do not feel at ease or work effectively with more than a dozen students at a time. With those dozen, however, they are unusually effective. There are other people who have a gift for working on a one-to-one basis with students no one else seems to reach. There are ways to prepare oneself for individual or small-group work—as skills specialist, remedial teacher, learning disabilities specialist, and so forth. There are also schools where it is possible to work with small groups as a teacher. Once you decide how you want to begin to work in a school, then you can look around and try to discover a situation in which you can be effective.

10. A final, though complex, question is what kind of school one should teach in. This is especially difficult for people like myself, who believe that almost every school in the United States, within and without the public school system, contributes to maintaining an oppressive society based upon an unequal distribution of wealth and a debasement of people's sense of dignity and personal worth. In the next section I will elaborate on this and suggest some ways of infiltrating the system and struggling to change it. It is my conviction that teachers who comply with the values and goals of this culture can only do so at the cost of stripping their students of self-respect and substituting violence in the form of competition in place of knowledge, curiosity, and a sense of community.

Getting a Job. There are not many teaching jobs these days. If you still care to teach, broaden your notion of where you might teach. The schools are only one possible place. Try businesses, social agencies, hospitals, parks, community service organizations.

It is, for example, possible to teach literacy to hospitalized children, to use an art and recreation program as a means of teaching most anything; to become associated with a job training program or a prison program. It is possible to set up a child care operation in your home, or turn babysitting into a teaching situation, or set up an after-school tutoring program. Often there are federal or state monies available for reading or child care or delinquency prevention programs. It is important to know how to get access to that money. If necessary, go to the county board of education, to Head Start offices, to regional offices of the Department of Health, Education and Welfare and ask about the programs they sponsor. Often a few weeks of research may open up a number of unexpected possibilities. The Grantsmanship Newsletter is an excellent source of information and is worth having (for subscriptions write to Grantsmanship Center, 1015 W. Olympic Blvd., Los Angeles, CA. 90015).

Also think about teaching children with problems—the severely disturbed, retarded, physically handicapped, deaf, or blind. Remember, children are children despite the way in which society labels them. Basically the same techniques and belief in the children's abilities work with all kinds of children. If there are special things one need learn, they are easy to master. The more one thinks of teaching outside the schools, the more imaginative one can be in searching for a job that will allow one to teach, or in defining a job and convincing others that it is worth supporting.

3. *THE CRAFT OF TEACHING*

TEACHING WELL INVOLVES different skills in different school settings. In a traditional classroom teaching well consists of being able to manage a large number of students who are required to master a preset and inflexible curriculum. To do this a teacher must be able to control the students with a minimum of conflict and keep them moving through standard texts or workbooks. Since all the students will be doing the same work, the faster and slower students must somehow be accommodated in a way that neither accelerates nor halts the moderate and orderly pace of work of the majority of the group. This modulation requires considerable skill, especially if the faster students are not to become bored and the slower ones rebellious.

Teaching in a traditional public school setting also requires that the teacher learn how to master an absurd amount of paperwork, administer tests, and grade student work at the same time as keeping the students quiet and busy. At its best, traditional teaching involves the ability to entertain the class, keep the students alert, and show them as a group interesting aspects of what they are supposed to learn.

Most traditional teachers who do not depend upon harsh discipline or appeal to higher authorities use certain skills—the glance, the occasional quip, the emphasis on rewarding those who work and isolating those who are malingerers or seeming troublemakers. The problem is that the curriculum has to be followed and the group structure maintained. The teacher can, at best, try to make the material and structure more palatable.

This type of classroom depends upon the personality of the teacher and the authority he or she commands within the school as a whole. The traditional teacher needn't know much about the subject he or she is supposed to teach—the text and teachers' manual tell you all you need to know. If a teacher knows a bit more than the text, or knows how to enliven it, so much the better. However, this is icing—the basic skills traditional teachers must master are those involving the management of bodies, space, and time. One must learn how to control the day.

Most public school administrators judge teachers on their ability to manage students, comply with directives, and avoid major discipline problems. Whether one's students learn anything or feel good is not relevant. Some students are expected to fail, and most are expected to be bored. This produces the contradictory situation young teachers can find themselves in. They believe that if a student fails or is bored, it is their responsibility to modify the curriculum, the classroom structure, or their own behavior in order to build a program that makes sense to the students. Yet these very modifications, done in order to improve their effectiveness with their students, cause them to be labeled bad teachers in the eyes of their supervisors and colleagues. To teach well, one must risk being rejected by many of the adults at one's school for caring too much about the students.

Teaching well from my perspective involves the skill and ingenuity to reconstruct the curriculum, redesign the environment, and change one's own behavior so that one's students will have the experiences, resources, and support they need to develop their sensitivity, compassion, and intelligence. This can be interpreted as being committed to open education or free education or child-centered learning. The labels are unimportant. What is crucial is the ability to observe and discover students' skills and needs, and build a learning environment that grows from them and does not violate them. A teacher has to be responsive to the students, rather than dependent upon a preset curriculum. It takes time and experience to observe and respond well with young people. No one starts out teaching well. Student teaching at its best just gives one a taste of what it is possible to do. Usually it just gives one exposure to a traditional, well-run, highly controlled classroom. The real struggle begins during the first year of teaching. As with any craft, it takes time and experience to feel comfortable and build up enough resources to deal with problems that arise unexpectedly. There are, however, ways to prepare oneself for the first few years of teaching. Here are some that have helped me in my own teaching and helping student teachers.

GATHERING RESOURCES

The more one knows and can do, the easier teaching will be. This is especially true in elementary school, where the teacher is supposed to cover a whole variety of subjects, or in open high schools, where the boundaries between the disciplines are often erased. Teachers colleges often make mistakes in spending so much time on theory and history of education and allowing their students so little time to learn things they care to teach. Some things prospective teachers might explore both for their own pleasure and because they might come in handy in class are:

a) Maps and mapmaking;

b) Toy making, especially balancing and moving toys that are useful in exploring physical principles such as gravity and inertia;

c) A whole range of crafts including candle making, leather work, macramé, bead making, ceramics, tie dyeing and batik, woodworking, photography (developing as well as taking pictures), woodcut and linoleum block printing, painting, drawing, cooking (especially in culturally different cuisines), auto and motorcycle repair, clothes making, weaving. The list can go on indefinitely. It is especially valuable if men try their hands at crafts our culture defines as woman's work and women try their hands at so-called men's work. Many students, seeing their teacher do the unexpected or nontraditional become bold themselves.

One thing must be emphasized: the teacher should work in these crafts and not merely read a manual on how to teach others to do them. Young people will naturally experiment more freely and creatively with painting, writing, and building if their teachers will also try their hands at the work than if the teacher just stands around and judges. Besides, trying to do something that is difficult and new is a healthy way for the teacher to keep in contact with the struggles to learn which his or her pupils encounter every day in school.

d) Music making, music listening, and music composition.

Listen to as wide a range of music as you can. Listen to the music your students like. You don't have to like it, but you have to respect it. Too many teachers make a moral hierarchy of music styles with classical music at the top and jazz somewhere at the bottom. That is fascist nonsense. If you cannot respect the tastes of people you work with, you probably ought to be teaching someone else.

e) Dance if you can, and observe people dancing and learning, teaching, and inventing new steps. What I said of music is true of dancing. I feel that an elementary school classroom without music or dancing that the students enjoy is lifeless.

f) Poetry—try to read some, especially modern works. Listen to recordings of poets reading their own works; write your own poems; read poetry aloud to your friends or into a tape recorder. The ability to read well to others and to tell stories is an invaluable skill in any teaching situation. I've never met a good teacher who didn't have something of the ancient storyteller in him or her. Young teachers are often shy in front of their students, and it takes a while to find one's voice with the class. However, ease comes after a while, especially if one develops a repertoire of stories that please one and are not learned because they're supposed to please young children.

g) Play around with math if you can. There are a number of delightful books that introduce mathematical games and recreations, as well as the practical uses of math. Martin Gardner's *Scientific American Book of Mathematical Puzzles and Diversions* (New York: Simon and Schuster, 1959) is a good book to start with. Some of the beauty of pure math can also be discovered through books like Rozsa Peter's *Playing with Infinity* (New York: Atheneum, 1969) and Harold Jacobs's *Mathematics: A Human Endeavor* (San Francisco: W. H. Freeman, 1970).

h) Learn to play games and try to make up some yourself. Also discover the games your students and their families play. Psychological games, as well as strategy games, should be studied. They provide good starting points for work in the classroom. A fine introductory book to games and gaming is Iona and Peter Opie's *Children's Games in Street and Playground* (London: Oxford, 1969). This book is a collection of children's games played throughout the British Isles, and yet the games it describes are

THE CRAFT OF TEACHING

probably universal, as one sees in the chapter headings: Chasing Games; Catching Games; Seeking Games; Hunting Games; Racing Games; Dueling Games; Daring Games; Guessing Games; and so forth.

The Center for Open Learning and Teaching, which I work with, has put out a number of booklets on the use of games in the classroom. One, *Your Move* by Ray Nitta, gives instructions on how to make and play a number of non-Western games. Another, which I wrote, is a manual on the history, rules, and strategies of chess written for elementary school children. The Center also publishes a monthly magazine on games called *GAMESEMAG*. The magazine ranges from language and math and logic games to superheroes. All of this material is available from the Center for Open Learning and Teaching, P.O. Box 9434, Berkeley, Calif. 94709.

There is a book put out by Oxford University Press in 1952 called *A History of Board-Games Other Than Chess,* by H. J. R. Murray. This book surveys board games that have originated throughout the world and organizes them into categories that are quite suggestive of subjects that go beyond the games themselves. For example, the book talks about games of alignment and configuration, war games, hunt games, race games, and so forth.

There are too many excellent books about the game of chess for me to mention any here. However, a fine introduction to the social and psychological symbolism of the chess game is presented in Vladimir Nabokov's novel, *Defense* (New York: Putnam, 1970).

Going beyond the games of the young and the amusements of the older, there is a group of books that have appeared recently that plays with the notion of games embodying psychological and social forms of behavior. Stephen Potter's *Complete Upmanship* (New York: Holt, Rinehart, 1971), Laurence Peter's *The Peter Principle* (New York: Morrow, 1969), C. Northcote Parkinson's *Parkinson's Law* (Boston: Houghton Mifflin, 1957), and Eric Berne's *Games People Play* (New York: Grove, 1964) are obvious examples of this genre.

There are some more serious, though perhaps less popular, studies of the games that people play when they meet each other face to face. R. D. Laing, in *Sanity, Madness and the Family* (New York: Basic, 1964), describes the kind of games that can drive people mad. He elaborates on this theme in *The Politics of Experience* (New York: Pantheon, 1967), and in *The Self and Others* (Chicago: Quadrangle, 1962).

Sociologist Erving Goffman talks about the form of social games played in prisons, mental institutions, and other institutions that pretend to totally control the lives of the inmates. *Asylums* (Chicago: Aldine, 1962) is his most accessible work. In another, *The Presentation of Self in Everyday Life* (Garden City, N.Y.: Doubleday, 1959), Goffman presents a theatrical theory of man's relation to other men. He tries to carry the analogy between life and the stage as far as possible, talking about the roles people play, and the behavior they exhibit offstage when the show is over, as well as describing the complexities of onstage behavior.

The analogy of life as a theatrical performance leads quite naturally to the study of the stage as a mirror of life. There are many interesting books on theater games, but so far as I am concerned *The Drama Review* (32 Washington Place, Room 73, New York, N.Y. 10003) is the most interesting and avant-garde journal I have seen. In it many of the games modern theater people play are presented and documented. Many games people imagine and yet don't dare to play are also described. I have found *The Drama Review* to be full of ideas that are readily usable in the classroom.

These days the theater has frequently moved out into the streets. Performances have taken place in supermarkets, at airports, in churches. The Happening, which merges painting, sculpture, environmental design, and theater into one total game has become increasingly accepted as a legitimate form of play. There are interesting books on Happenings that are worth looking at. First, there is Allan Kaprow's *Assemblages, Environments & Happenings* (New York: Abrams, 1966). Then there is Michael Kirby's *Happenings* (New York: Dutton, 1966). The Something Else Press, run by Dick Higgins in New York, puts out a whole series of books on Happenings, events, games, and other contemporary forms of celebration. George Brecht and Robert Filliou's *Games at the Cedilla* (New York: Something Else, 1967) is a good introduction to the playful form of madness that has been popularized more recently by John Lennon, the Beatles, and Yoko Ono.

Games generally have rules and players. In this sense language is one of the most complex of games. There are several interesting introductions to language games. Ludwig Wittgenstein's *Blue and Brown Books* (Oxford: Blackwell, 1958) and *Philosophical Investigations* (New York: Macmillan, 1958) are difficult, yet interesting, studies of language as a series of interrelating games. They are full of examples of games that students can play in order to grasp the nature of learning to speak.

There are also simpler books—e.g., Lancelot Hogben's *The Mother Tongue* (New York: Norton, 1964)—which deal with language and the way it is used, as well as with its developmental history.

i) Science can be explored in everyday life. The study of television, cars, radios, stoves, refrigerators, door bells, lights, the sewer system, the flush toilet, the sink, the heating system, the structure of a home or school all provide rich, open-ended topics to explore with one's students. However, most of us don't know how TV works or why the toilet flushes. We should learn ourselves or with our students.

j) History need not be the study of remote people during forgotten times (though this can be interesting and important too). Do a history of your own family, of your neighbors, of the objects you own and use, of the building you live in. Do the same with your students. Tell them what you've discovered about yourself and use your experience as a starting point. Your students are usually more curious about you than you are about them.

k) Pursue any academic subject—archaeology, anthropology, sociology, chemistry, German literature—anything that interests you, and then try to bring it closer and closer to your everyday life and then to the lives of your students. Try to translate what you know and care about into terms that make sense to them. Then they will probably do the same for you and teach you.

Teachers should also know something about helping students learn how to help others. The National Commission on Resources for Youth (36 West 44th Street, New York, N.Y. 10036) publishes a free quarterly newsletter and distributes videotapes, films, and books about students helping each other and their communities. It is worth getting on their mailing list and using their material.

TOOLS FOR TEACHING

Learn to use the tools needed to make your own curriculum. At a minimum, this means knowing how to use woodworking tools (especially power drills and saws), a sewing machine, a rexograph machine, and a small hand press. Bookmaking and printmaking are also useful skills. I have found that most expensive educational materials can be redesigned and constructed inexpensively. One way to get ideas for classroom materials is to collect educational, toy, and scientific catalogues and make your own versions of what looks interesting. These catalogues usually tell enough about the material that one can figure out how to use them.

A small shop in your home is useful. Most serious teachers spend time at home making materials, posters, and so forth. A paper cutter, X-acto knives, a saddle stitch stapler (to bind small books inexpensively), paper and wood glues, a glue gun, woodworking tools, a hole puncher, a T-square and 30/60/90 and 45/90 triangles, needles and thread, wood, cloth and plastic scraps, paper, pens, and paints provide all the equipment needed to build most of what you need in school. Two or three teachers could easily put together such a shop in a basement or garage or corner of a room and use it as their own mini-theater resource center. If you do this, it is a good idea to make an extra sample of everything to keep in the shop so other teachers can share what you invent or create. In this way a whole repertoire of useful material can develop.

Some books which illustrate useful techniques are: *Creative Bookbinding*, Pauline Johnson (Seattle: Univ. of Washington Press, 1973); *How to Work With Wood and Tools*, edited by Robert Campbell (New York: Pocket Books, 1975); *Apparatus: A Source Book of Information and Ideas*, F. F. Blackwell (New York: Agathon, 1967); *The Whole Word Catalogue* (Teachers and Writers Collaborative, New York, 1972). This last book is available from the Teachers and Writers Collaborative, c/o P.S. 3, 490 Hudson St., New York, N.Y. 10014.

DEVELOPING A CURRICULUM THEME

There are some useful techniques that can help develop all the material and skills you accumulate into curriculum themes that can be used in very flexible ways in the classroom. Instead of focusing on a particular technique or a single subject area, it is better to focus on a broad and interesting theme such as power, or love, or walls, or magic, or monsters, or moving to a new place, and then develop it. Several years ago I decided to begin with the theme "circus-time" and develop it as preparation for the school year.

I chose the theme because the circus is magic to almost all of us. It combines danger and discipline, involves encountering and taming the wild and at times death itself, and combines farce and high seriousness. It encompasses so many different aspects of life and fantasy that it is very rare to find a student completely indifferent to the circus.

Before introducing the theme of the circus to my class I did two things. First, I went to the circus to remind myself what it was all about. Then I did some analysis of what I saw and speculated upon things that could be studied in conjunction with the circus. In that way I planned a series of activities, projects, and demonstrations for the class, developed a number of starting points, and came up with a whole range of topics that could be explored depending upon the students' interests. As a way of starting out my planning, I wrote the word "circus" on the middle of a blank sheet of paper and then wrote down different aspects of the circus as they occurred to me:

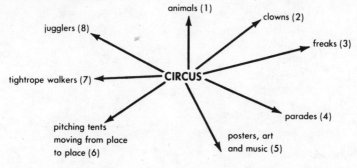

animals (1)

clowns (2)

jugglers (8)

freaks (3)

tightrope walkers (7) ← CIRCUS

parades (4)

pitching tents
moving from place
to place (6)

posters, art
and music (5)

Then I looked at each of these subthemes and began to develop them in the same way, this time, however, getting both more particular in terms of activities that can be used in the classroom, and more general with respect to other areas that could be studied taking off from these aspects of the circus. In order to do this I started again with a blank piece of paper with the theme written down in the middle of the sheet. For example, the theme of animals in the circus was developed in the following way:

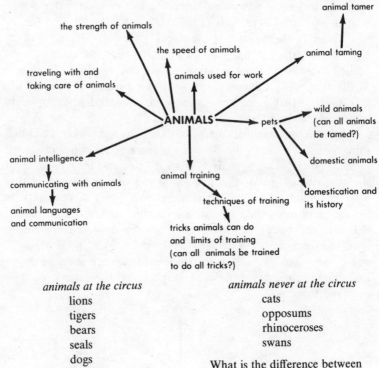

animals at the circus
lions
tigers
bears
seals
dogs
monkeys
elephants
horses
dolphins
parrots

What are the different
functions of these animals?

animals never at the circus
cats
opposums
rhinoceroses
swans

What is the difference between
those at the circus and those not?

Another subtheme whose development I would like to illustrate is tightrope walking, which I found more convenient to turn into the theme of balancing in general. Occasionally, rephrasing the theme in a more general way leads to more associations and ideas than something as particular as walking the tightrope.

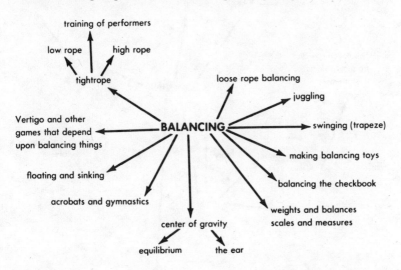

The subthemes juggling and swinging, can also be elaborated in the same way.

Another rich theme, perhaps my favorite, is clowns as shown on page 40.

There is no exhaustive way to treat any of these themes. Any rich web of associations and ideas is enough of a beginning. After developing the initial theme and elaborating a number of sub-themes it helps to get more specific and prepare classroom activities in one or two of the areas you want to use in class first. As an example of how this can be done, take the theme of balancing and the diagram that represents ways of using the theme. Each of the arrows represents a whole area that can be explored in class. Each of these, in turn, can be explored in greater depth, and specific

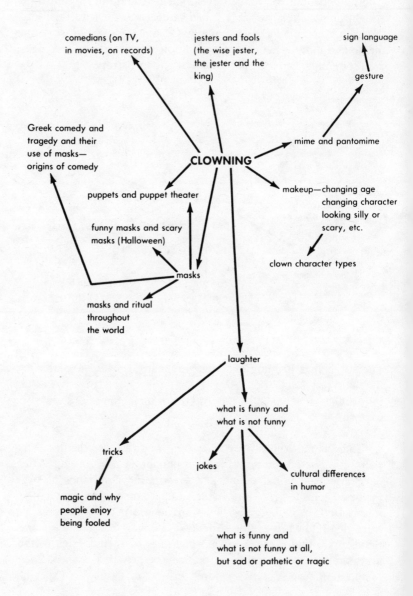

comedians (on TV, in movies, on records)

jesters and fools (the wise jester, the jester and the king)

sign language

gesture

Greek comedy and tragedy and their use of masks— origins of comedy

mime and pantomime

CLOWNING

puppets and puppet theater

makeup—changing age changing character looking silly or scary, etc.

funny masks and scary masks (Halloween)

masks

clown character types

masks and ritual throughout the world

laughter

what is funny and what is not funny

tricks

jokes

cultural differences in humor

magic and why people enjoy being fooled

what is funny and what is not funny at all, but sad or pathetic or tragic

activities for classroom use can be enumerated. In my notes I
elaborated on some of them:

    1. Making balancing toys—
        a) See MacDonald book on *Science Through Toys*
        b) Out of knitting needles, corks, and clay make toys that can
balance on a rope or pin or finger. These are just like tightrope walkers.
See illustration:

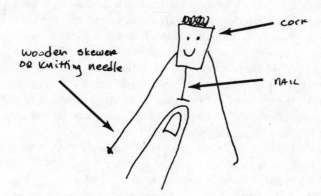

        c) Make a seesaw and things that balance each other on it
        d) Go to a toy store and look at all the commercial balancing toys.
Is there any way to make them cheaply with material already available?
        e) Play around with balanced structures with Lego blocks and with
G-Stix and see how the geodesic dome and triangular structures can make
large, rigid, and balanced structures. Possibly you can get into the study of
bridges here but is this taking the circus a bit too far? Look at portable
tents and cages that are actually used—there might be a connection here.
    2. Tightrope walking—the rigid rope—
        a) Experiment with having the students walk a straight line marked
out on the floor, then walk on blocks, then on chairs. Watch what they do
to balance and keep themselves going. Does a long, bent, heavy pole help
as they walk on higher surfaces?
        b) Talk about fear of heights. How does feeling about the
performance affect the performance? Maybe you can get into the whole
question of confidence here. You can think up a number of writing topics
dealing with times students were confident and times they were afraid.
        c) There is a great scope for improvisation here. Have students
improvise walking the wire 100 feet up, have others be the audience and

the relatives of the performers. Have the performer falter, and even fall. Do improvisations of young performers about to go up on the high wire for the first time being reassured by the old-timers, and so forth.

d) You can also measure the actual heights of the tightwire, and look at the differences in the low and high wires. And you can measure the heights the students are used to climbing. This might be a good way to begin to study the question of height in general.

All of this may seem like an awful lot of teacher preparation. It certainly involves more time and research than what usually goes into making up lesson plans. However, there are rewards. You learn an enormous amount yourself as these ideas develop, and you come up with more material than can ever be used during one school year. There is always enough left over for the next year, for the next group of students who will likely have different interests and take the study of the theme in a different direction. The next time through you will not be repeating things, but dealing with the same wealth of material in a new and unpredictable way.

Once all the material has been gathered and the theme developed, it is important to think of ways of introducing the subject to your students.

There is no single best way to begin teaching a theme, and the way it is introduced will depend to a large degree upon the resources available. In the case of the circus, it would be natural to think about it in the classroom somewhere around the time that the circus is making a visit to your community. Some teachers might want to begin when ads appear in the paper and study the circus before it actually arrives, ending the unit with a class visit to the circus. Others might want to make the visit first and let the classroom activities and discussions come out of the children's experience with the real thing. A third way might be to work a circus visit in somewhere during the middle of the unit. I was lucky in that one of my former students attended the Ringling Brothers Clown College in Sarasota, Florida, and he was able to come to class and show us some of his clown faces and some tricks. Then he told us about traveling with the circus and we were on our way. We followed his trip with a study of clown faces, with making up the students and having them evolve their own clown characters, and with listening to a shortened version of the opera *Pagliacci* and talking about sad clowns and the masks they wore. From that we studied and made masks and did some short plays with masked superheroes that the students made up.

It is always fine to have someone from the circus world come to class and talk to the children. There are many people who have performed in county fairs and small circuses who would be willing to volunteer. Local theater groups, the actors' union, local carnival performers, and actors at college all are possible sources of people to come and make theater real for the class.

For some teachers it is not possible to use the immediate experience of the circus. There are still many interesting ways to bring up the subject in class. For example, one can start by decorating the class with old circus posters. These are readily available from Ringling Brothers. There is also a book full of colorful old circus posters that can be cut up and displayed *(100 Years of Circus Posters,* Jack Rennert, New York: Avon, 1974). It is possible to begin by discussing the posters and asking students if they ever went to the circus. Then one can develop with the class a diagram similar to the one used in researching the theme in the first place and put down all the aspects of the circus that the students remembered. A diagram I developed with a group of first-graders looked like this:

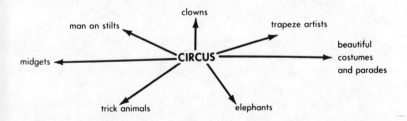

From this diagram it is possible to move in a number of ways. Groups could be formed to study the different aspects of the circus and could also be formed to rehearse and perform part of a class circus. I have found that when something like the circus is studied, no matter how far one ranges into related areas of study, it is always satisfying to the students to end the unit with a performance.

There are at least two types of circus the class can create. One is a circus with the students as performers. This could even involve them in training animals and bringing their own pets that can do tricks or be dressed up for a parade. It is easy to develop a clown show (see Viola Spolin's *Improvisation for the Theater,* Evanston, Ill., Northwestern University Press, 1963, for ideas), to practice some magic tricks and juggling tricks. Some students can do tumbling and balancing, and usually one can find a few musicians or at least a drummer to accompany the performers.

It is also possible and fun to build a model circus with balancing toys and clowns, puppets, papier-mâché animals, and carts and other vehicles that can move and be made to parade and even do tricks. The students can make and perform this miniature circus for other classes and parents, and since the miniature circus is quite portable, it can be taken to other classes for performances. There are a number of sources for ideas and models of things to include in the portable circus:

> *Calder's Circus,* edited by Jean Lipman (New York: Dutton and the Whitney Museum of American Art, 1972);
> *Play With Paper,* Thea Bank-Jensen (New York: Macmillan, 1962
> *Paper Folding for Beginners,* William Murray and Francis Rigney (New York: Dover, 1960);
> *Puppet Party,* by Goldie Tau Chernoff (Scholastic Book Service, 1972).

Other ways to introduce the circus theme might be to put on a record of circus music or have the class watch Burt Parks's TV show on the circus or have the class draw pictures of what the circus looked like to them,

It is also possible to start by introducing a narrow aspect of circus life and then, after a while, build up to studying the circus as a whole. For example, one can start by showing the class Oscar the balancing cork-man (illustrated on page 00). Oscar will balance on the tip of a finger, on a rope, on the corner of a table or book, or even on the tip of your nose. The whole topic of balances and scales can then be introduced simply by showing Oscar and having the class make their own dolls, adjusting the arms and the clay so that they balance. It is possible to point out to students that the tightrope walker uses a pole in much the way Oscar uses his arms—to lower the center of balance or gravity below the rope and, therefore, insure greater stability. From here it is possible to discuss the combination of science and skill that makes up the design of circus tricks.

It is also possible to start by talking about the students' pets and the things they can be trained to do. From there one can move to a discussion of animal training in general, and then it is a small step to the circus.

Another specific thing one can do is begin with a magic trick or juggling trick. I like to use magic tricks since they immediately rivet students' attention, pose a problem in terms of figuring how the trick works, and can lead in any number of directions. My favorite beginning tricks are sleight-of-hand tricks that can be done with sponge rubber balls. The tricks involve concealing one or two balls in the palm and then making the balls seem to multiply or come out of people's mouths or ears or noses or pockets. These balls and instructions for the tricks are available in most toy stores.

Once after showing my class some sleight-of-hand magic, I explained to them that much magic attempted to trick their eyes. Then I showed them some visual illusions that did the same thing.

Which line is longer?

See the duck?
See the rabbit?
(Turn the book sideways to the right.)

Finally, I showed them a flip book and illustrated how the eye can be tricked into seeing movement where there is none. From there the students leaped to the idea of making flip books themselves by drawing pictures on the bottom of a pad and making each picture slightly different. Then one of the students asked if that was how people made real movies, and a few days later I brought in a film and showed the class how, indeed, motion pictures are a form of visual illusion. From there we went on to study and make films. In order to get back to the circus, I brought up the idea of doing an animated film about a magician and suggested that the magician be part of a magic circus. If the students didn't like my pushing them in that direction, I would have shifted strategy and asked them what they wanted to film. There are times that the best of one's teaching ideas don't get used because the students are more interested in other things, and one should simply not destroy or interfere with that curiosity and enthusiasm. One must follow the lead of the students, even if occasionally it takes one away from what is familiar, comfortable, or even exciting to one as a teacher and learner. Besides, there is usually time to return to things during the year, and there is always next year with another group of young people with different interests.

Here are a few themes that were developed by Cris Evans, a teacher at the Family School in Cedar Rapids, Iowa.

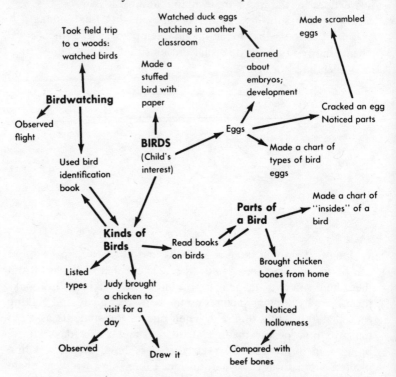

This was a project of one child; it developed from her interests.

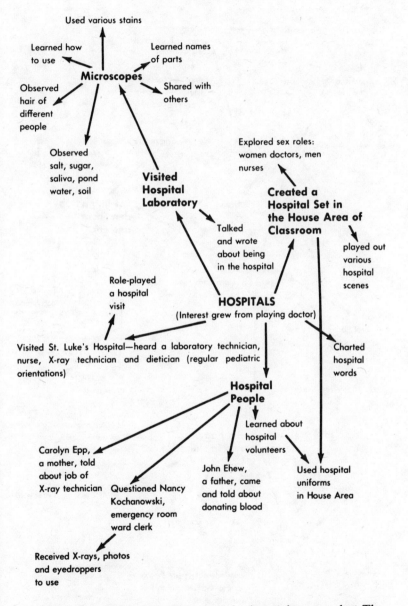

A group project—four kids—lasted about three weeks. The whole class took the pediatric orientation hospital trip.

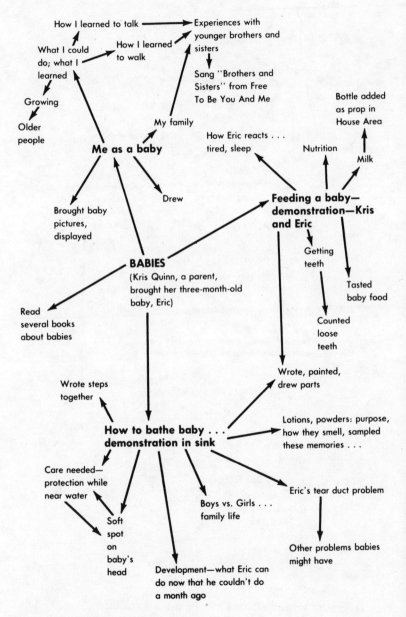

A one-day, whole-class project.

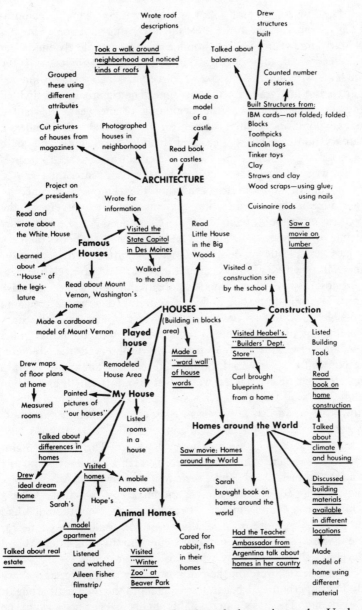

Houses theme with whole class lasted about six weeks. Underlined activities everyone participated in.

The kind of planning represented by these thematic elabora-
tions is crucial, even in the most open learning situations. One has
to start somewhere. The classroom cannot be completely empty nor
the teacher devoid of ideas and starting experiences for the
students without inviting chaos. Three years ago I taught kindergarten and first grade for the first time. The classroom was divided
into learning centers at the beginning of the year. We had a
bookmaking and reading center, an art and craft shop center, a
fantasy house, a block area, and a center for science and math
games. Except for the times when the class was together for stories
or for writing, the students could choose which center they wanted
to be in. In addition to organizing the centers, I planned to
introduce a theme which the students could explore in all the
centers and which might bring the class together. The beginning
theme of the year was *Dinosaurs and Monsters.* I got books on these
topics, got plastic models, costumes, and art materials to make
imaginary beasts. I found a dinosaur poster that gave relative sizes
of dinosaurs and other animals, made up dinosaur games and flash
cards. I studied the topic myself, developed a whole range of
possible directions to move in, started by reading a monster story
the first day of school. The poster was on the wall, the books in the
reading center. From that point on, I observed the students'
responses to the material. Some were curious about how long a
brontosaurus really was, so we measured out its length and height
along the wall outside our classroom. The students didn't know
how to use a yardstick, so measurement was worked in. Somehow
we got into discussions about nightmares and made pictures, told
dreams, and put nightmare books together. The words "nightmare," "monster," "dinosaur" were written everywhere, and the
students copied them, and labeled their drawings. A nightmare
play developed—costumes, sets, and make-up included. After a
while, monsters and dinosaurs became boring, even though I had
prepared a lot more material than ever was used. It was time for
me to introduce another theme or follow the students' interests and
develop a theme related to what was on their minds.

Superheroes were on their minds during the spring, and so we
studied superheroes. I began thinking about the theme after one of
David and Thomas's interminable fights over who was to be
Batman and who was to be Robin. Cheryl joined in, offering to be

Robin, and Thomas compromised by choosing to become Superman and leaving Batman to David. The three superheroes flew off. David was black, Cheryl was black and female, and Thomas was white; yet in their superhero modes they were all white males. I wondered if they were aware of that fact or troubled by it.

After school that day I bought a dozen comic books and did a racial and sexual count of superheroes. My casual survey came up with nine white male superheroes (Batman, Superman, Submariner, Aquaman, Spiderman, Captain America, Shazaam, Flash, and Green Lantern) and one white female superhero (Wonderwoman). Falcon was the only black superhero, and he was Captain America's sidekick, though recently he has been achieving more independent status. The next day I brought the comics to class, and during story time laid the books out on the floor. All of the students, who are five and six years old, were familiar with the characters in these books and started chatting about their favorites. Although the class is half black and half white, none of the students identified with Falcon because he was a second-rate hero. All of the students wanted to be the strongest and most intelligent superhero possible. They wanted power and were willing to cross racial and sexual lines to identify with it.

I suggested that we change the superheroes and imagine a Spider Woman or Superwoman. One of the girls mentioned that there already was a Super Girl, but she wasn't as powerful as Superman. Superwoman was a whole new idea—a female coequal of Superman, not merely a sidekick or a child. Some boys felt the idea was silly—there just couldn't be a woman as powerful as Superman. I pressed the issue—why not? "Because boys are tougher than girls," the boys yelled. However, in our class the biggest and toughest student was a girl, Cheryl. The facts and the stereotypes simply didn't match.

It was as hard for some of the girls to accept Superwoman as for the boys. The idea of such a forceful and independent woman made them uneasy. They preferred the role of Lois Lane, the mortal woman in love with the male superhero, Superman.

There were similar problems with changing the complexions of the superheroes. A black or brown Superman, Batman, or Wonderwoman didn't seem right to many of the students. Most of the white students just put the idea down as one of Herb's silly ideas. A number of the black students were more distressed—the idea was tempting and yet made them feel uneasy. One of the black students challenged my transformations and sex change operations. He said that whatever I said, he knew there were really no black super-heroes. Fortunately, I had a copy of a comic book drawn by one of my former students a few years before. The main character was Combinative Man, a black superhero who had power of mind and power of soul. On his utility belt he had a power reflecting mirror that could hypnotize people and call forth mirages and illusions that Combinative Man willed. In one of the episodes I read to the class, Combinative Man frightened off his enemies by producing imaginary monsters and beasts, which they took for real.

Combinative Man convinced the students that black super-heroes existed. The next day Darryle, the boy who had challenged me, came to class with a mirror in his belt. He was Combinative Man.

I suggested that the students write their own comic books and create their own superheroes. We agreed that the heroes we created had to represent the whole class, male and female, black and white. Instead of starting with comic book creatures and modifying them slightly, we began by listing the powers the students wanted their heroes to assume. The list included the power to: see through things; know what someone else was thinking; speak to animals; knock down buildings; change into animals; fly; swim under water; burrow tunnels in the ground; and make people have nightmares.

One of the boys came up with the Mauler, a person with six arms, giant fists, and a small body that could stretch like silly putty. Another made up the Listener, who could hear everything in the world and travel with the speed of light. Cathleen made up a superhero who looked like an ordinary girl, but could talk to animals, change into their forms, or use any of their powers at will.

My daughter, Tonia, who was in the class, made up Cancer-girl since she is born under the astrological sign of Cancer. Cancer-girl could pinch like a crab, live in the sea and on land, and burrow under things. She had hard skin that no bullet or knife could pierce and antennas that could pick up smells miles away.

Tonia's selection of her astrological sign led a number of other students to look to astrology for inspiration. We had a number of archers, Toroman, and Cappy, a superhero mountain goat who could climb up buildings and eat through any material.

The students created their own comic books. I encouraged them to work in small groups, help each other with spelling and drawing, and talk together about story lines. Whenever anyone needed a word to be spelled, I supplied it. Some students wanted to draw and so they dictated the dialogue, which I wrote down for them. The Mauler and the Listener worked together, as did Cancer-girl, Cappy, and Toroman. Sometimes the superheroes were friends fighting a common enemy. At other times they opposed each other, matching one superpower against another. I was struck by how much thought the students put into defining the powers their heroes had and exploring the consequences of having that power. It was as if I had provided a vehicle the students could use to explore becoming powerful adults in their own individual ways.

The students read their comic books to each other, made costumes for themselves and played at being these characters both formally and informally. There were complicated fantasy games going on for a while where alliances of heroes were created and superpowers displayed. There were also plays the students wrote and performed for each other involving battles of superheroes against dinosaurs or creatures from outer space.

After a while, I introduced a new element into the students' thinking about superheroes—that of traditional mythology. I told stories of the Greek and Mesoapotamian gods, showed the students pictures of Hindu godfigures, read from *Orisha,* which is about the gods and heroes of the Yoruba of Nigeria *(Orisha: The Gods of Yorubaland,* Judith Gleason, New York: Atheneum, 1971), introduced the students to stories about the lives and powers of Egyptian and Chinese gods and heroes. From comic books centered on white male heroes of twentieth-century America, we moved to the children's own creations and then beyond that to the gods, male and female, black, brown, yellow, red, and white that people have created for centuries to represent powers they had or aspired to, and to explore through stories and tales the consequences of having or desiring power.

This all happened at the end of the school year, and so things were terminated abruptly. However, after exploring mythology, a number of students returned to their own creations and changed them, borrowing freely from the world's myths, developing more elaborate stories. This interplay of the students' ideas with material outside their immediate experience led to stories that could not have developed through the children's imagination alone or through teaching mythology and ignoring the students' inspiration. Both seem to me to be necessary for sustained creative work.

For me planning consisted of balancing teacher-initiated ideas with student-initiated ones, of doing research as a teacher, and observing and responding to what actually succeeded with the students. This is quite different from following a set curriculum or using standard texts, and involves *planning, research, observation,* and *response,* which are basic skills of the craft of teaching.

Some other themes we explored during the year were:

> magic, illusion, and the phenomenon of light;
> the Ashanti culture as an introduction to Africa—the theme was an Ashanti saying: "Do everything well, make everything beautiful";
> power—electricity, bulbs, batteries, lights, doorbells;
> mapping, from the classroom through the world, with a discussion of driving a car, finding one's way home, discovering where one's parents and ancestors were born, making up imaginary cities and countries, and so on.

There is a whole series of science curriculum books produced in England that are based on the notion of introducing a theme and developing it according to students' responses. This is the *Macdonald Education Science/5-13* series and cover such themes as science through toys, holes, gaps, and cavities, ourselves, structures and forces, change, and more. The books can be obtained through Macdonald Educational, 49-50 Poland Street, London W1, or in the United States through European Publishers Representatives, 11-03 46th Ave., Long Island City, New York 11101.

INTEGRATING THE CURRICULUM

When developing and introducing a theme, it is important to keep in mind that different subject areas such as math, reading, science, history, and so forth are only kept separate at the cost of diminishing what can be learned. The compartmentalization of knowledge, which begins as early as primary school, is often considered so natural that it isn't questioned. In most schools subjects such as language arts and history and arithmetic are separated from each other. Time is allocated to each subject and often no attempt is made to relate them to each other or to the general ways in which man comes to know and live with himself and his environment. Students get the impression that science is one thing and art something wholly different.

Textbooks and teachers' manuals enforce this fragmentation of learning. Students have science texts, math texts, reading texts, and history texts. When teachers who depend upon textbooks move from one area of knowledge to another, they have their students close one textbook, put it away in their desks, pause for a moment, and then take out another textbook.

Thinking and creating in science, the arts, mathematics is not that different. Scientist and artist alike try to understand aspects of reality, to conceive of important problems posed by life or the world and then to bring all their human faculties, intuitive as well as rational, to bear upon producing a solution or creating an explanation or embodying a thought or a feeling. They may focus their attention upon different aspects of reality, but their ways of thinking are not radically different. There are mathematicians whose thoughts are essentially poetic and poets whose works are mathematical. There are degrees of intuition, rationality, boldness, caution, grandness, or meticulousness in all creative thinkers. The more schools separate areas of thought, the more they encourage young people not to think in any of them.

It is not difficult to bring the curriculum together and break down the barriers between subject areas. Recently I was looking through a series of science curriculum guides produced by the Science Curriculum Improvement Study. These guides are based on discovery principles, i.e., on the notion that the student learns best when he discovers things for himself rather than being told them or reading them in a book. They provide a first step away from textbooks, though in my mind they do not go far enough since they determine what it is a student ought to discover.

However, they are well done and worth looking at. I was struck by how limited these guides became by being confined to the sciences. I would like to take some of the specific units and speculate upon how they can involve more than what is narrowly construed as science. The ones I will consider are titled *Interactions, Relativity, Systems and Subsystems,* and *Environments.*

Interactions can be looked upon as a study of the relationships between physical objects. It can also be looked upon as a study of the relationship between individuals (psychology), groups (sociology), nations (history), and ideas (philosophies). Interactions can be danced out, developed in improvisational drama, or studied in literature or the mass media. Culture, for example, can be considered the product of people interacting with nature. Hair styles can be studied as results of people transforming something natural (hair) into a symbol of status and identity. Clothes and cars and furniture can be looked at in the same way. A good way to begin this way of studying interactions is to look at the hair and dress styles of all the people in the class (teacher included) and try to discover how they developed.

Relativity need not be confined to relativity physics. One can study moral principles and values, examine the relativity of cultures, get into listening to different musical systems (eight-tone, five-tone, twelve-tone) and even into creating musical instruments and systems whose value is relative to other musical systems. One can also study relatives (I'm his cousin, he's my cousin, but I'm his uncle and he's my nephew) and then kinship systems. One can also talk about looking at the world through other eyes and trying to understand the experience of other people and creatures. One can dance out the movement of two independent systems moving with relationship to each other.

Systems and Subsystems. Think of a jazz combo as a system with several subsystems—one, for example, the rhythm section and another (within the rhythm section) the subsystem of drums and cymbals. Listen to the musical group as a whole and then listen to the subsystems. Or again take a game like football—think of the whole team, the offense, the defense, the linemen, the quarterback, the running backs. Play the game and look at films of the game the way you would look at a system to be studied in physics. Then look at the game as a dance. Move from one mode of perception and thought to another. The free play of imagination and intellect is certainly one of the components of creative thought in any discipline.

Environments. One can study physical environment. One can also create environments. Recently I worked with a group of youngsters who created a suburb out of cardboard tubes, string, and paper. As we developed the suburb we became the residents of our environment and acted out the lives of the people we had created.

Using the simplest and cheapest materials, one can recreate the world in the classroom. One can also look at contemporary art, at the environments of Andy Keinholtz, Claes Oldenburg, and Allan Kaprow. One can study theater as a means of creating a simulated environment.

So far I have started with a science theme and moved away from science into history and the arts. Recently I had a reverse experience with a group of students I was working with. We started out by telling a collective story—one line each. As the story evolved, the main characters found themselves in difficult positions and escaped by transforming themselves into animals. I followed the theme of transformation by suggesting that we all transform ourselves into anything we cared to and write a tale of a description from the point of view of the creature we became. The students became cats, flies, caterpillars, and in one case a boiling potato.

After writing, we drew pictures of the world through the eyes of our creature selves and then did an improvisation. We physically became the creatures we were transformed into and had to relate to each other.

From the transformation of ourselves we began to talk about magical transformation of physical objects. This naturally led to alchemy and from there to chemistry. This whole experience led me to understand chemistry in a new and exciting way and restored some of the magic of chemical change that had been lost for me in school through the tedious memorizing of formulas and facts.

The elements of early science and alchemy can be profitably explored in greater depth. To the ancients, all of nature was made up of four elements—earth, air, fire, and water. These elements were the subject of scientific investigation; they were represented in paintings and described and invoked in poetry and music. Even today all of us have associations with these elements and preferences for one or the other of them. These associations and preferences can be used as a handle for opening up your classroom.

I begin by telling my students about the elements and the way in which some people felt they constituted the world. Then I ask the students to freely associate with each of the elements and put their associations on the board. Something like this usually results:

Earth: warm, dirty, seed, brown, rich green.
Air: thin, pure, fly, high, colorless, open, head.
Fire: heat, burn, hurt, passion, feel, love, die.
Water: swim, cool, drown, float, calm, storm.

Then we talk about the associations and about the differences that exist among the elements. After a while I ask the students to put down in order the elements they feel closest to. I do the same thing myself. Then we look at the class responses and see what our preferences are. The students look at each other's responses. There are no right and wrong answers—it is all a matter of personal preference. The elements simply tell the students things about themselves and each other.

One time a student suggested we make a chart of first preferences. It was interesting that in the class most of the boys preferred air and fire, and most of the girls preferred earth and water. For the Greeks air and fire were masculine elements, and earth and water, feminine.

After we examined everyone's preferences, I asked the class to assume that they were each composed of some mixture of earth, air, fire, and water and to make up charts of their own percentages. The students really got into thinking about themselves and became curious about each other's choices. Later, a student suggested that someone in the class leave the room and make up a chart about himself in the hall while everyone else made up their own charts on him. Then we could compare what the person thought of himself with how others perceived him (see table on the next page).

I made no attempt to interpret what the students said about each other and themselves. They understood certain things and

Jenny—Three Perceptions		
	Jenny sees herself	Teacher sees Jenny	Jon sees Jenny
Earth	10%	25%	10%
Air	10%	25%	10%
Fire	50%	25%	30%
Water	30%	25%	50%

accepted the exercises as nonjudgmental. There were no right or wrong responses, no marks involved. It was fun; they looked at each other and also at me as a person responding in the same way they responded. The students were able to get away from being passive in the classroom and from competing with each other.

I have used a series of differently colored cards in the same way, substituting color preference for element preference.

There are other ways to open up the classroom to spontaneity. Viola Spolin's *Improvisation for the Theater* is a rich source of ideas for improvisations. The improvisations that worked best with my classes are the ones that involved everyone, and not those that involve a small number of students performing for the rest of the class. One of my favorite forms of improvisation—I learned it from Viola Spolin's book—consists of:

1. Sending a student or a group of students out of the room.
2. Having the class develop a dramatic situation in which the people out of the room have a central role.
3. Getting everyone in the class involved in the set situations and . . .
4. Having the students in the hall return to the room, figure out the roles they are to play and then get involved in playing out those roles.

For example, everyone in the room can be an animal in the forest and the students in the hall can be huntsmen; or the students in the room can be devils and the ones in the hall new arrivals in hell; or the persons in the hall can be visitors to a wax museum and the ones in the classroom dummies made of wax.

An interesting variation on this last idea developed in one of my classes. One of our students discovered that in the San Francisco Wax Museum there is an actor made up to look like a wax dummy. His job is to move when people aren't looking—thus adding a bit of mystery and a touch of the supernatural to the exhibit. In our improvisation everyone in the room was a person made up to look like a wax figure. The students chose their roles and moved only when the "visitors" were not looking.

Techniques like these are meant to get the teacher out of the center of the room, and to get students to pay attention to each other and to value each other's ideas and actions. The central characteristic of these techniques is that they are noncompetitive, that they involve everyone in the class, including the teacher, in participating, and that they do not end in some form of judgment. They are interesting for their own sake, and because of that can bring people closer together.

Another way to get out of the center of the class and enable students to think for themselves and explore their environments is to observe animals in their natural environments instead of reading about them or seeing them in the zoo. Think of how unnaturally creatures behave in confinement: the big cats pace back and forth endlessly; the birds of prey sit chained to trees; the alligators and turtles lie dormant in a small pool of water surrounded by a fence. The zoo is a condition of life that modifies their behavior. They cannot be natural in unnatural circumstances. Yet most of the science that is taught in school and done in laboratories involves the manipulation of things in unnatural settings. We have to learn how to let things be, how to understand and respect things in their environments without destroying them. One way to begin is by learning how to observe some living thing without trying to control it or interfere in its life.

Think of an insect that lives in your environment. Suppose you choose an ant. How could you and your students learn about its life? One way would be to capture it and watch how it functions in a jar. This would be a bad choice because an ant cannot live and perform its ordinary life functions without being part of a community of ants. It would die of aloneness.

Another way to study the ant would be to simply look at it. That is not as easy as it sounds. To follow a single ant with your eyes and not lose it under a leaf or get it confused with the other ants around it takes intense concentration. I have tried myself, first for a few seconds at a time, and then gradually building up to five or ten minutes. I've also tried the same thing with my first-graders, who thought the whole thing was a joke until they began to realize how tired you can get by simply watching.

All of us had to learn how to slow down and quiet down, how to keep from being distracted. It was almost a form of meditation.

After following a single ant, we decided to chart its time and map the distance it covered. We drew pictures of its trail and made notes of each time it stopped to pick up a piece of food or to fight or help another ant. Then I raised the question: are all ants alike? How can you tell them apart without marking them in some way?

This involved us in a different form of observation since it was physical appearance and temperament we looked at rather than movement. Some ants were small and others very large. One of the students noticed that some of the ants had broken limbs or antennae; another observed that some moved faster than others and always seemed to be fighting.

I could have gone from the observation of ants into an analysis of the structure of ant communities and the anatomy of ants. However, the phenomenon of observing seemed more interesting, and so I introduced the class to Jakob von Uexkull's essay "A Stroll Through the Worlds of Animals and Men: A Picture Book of Invisible Worlds" (reprinted in *Instinctive Behavior,* edited by Claire H. Schiller, New York, International Universities Press, 1957). In this essay there is a series of pictures of an oak tree viewed from the perspective of many different creatures. The pictures show the oak tree as perceived by a woodsman, a scared little child, a fox, an owl, an ant, a bark beetle, and an ichneumon fly. In each case the tree is perceived and experienced in a different manner. I asked the class to think of what a tree means to an animal that lives in its roots as opposed to one that lives in its branches; to think of the size of the tree from the ant's perspective, and of its mystical powers as projected by the scared child. Then we shifted our discussion from observing things to getting into the minds of others and trying to learn how they perceived their world.

Drawing is a wonderful tool here. We drew pictures of a person from the perspective of a bird, a dog, a mouse. And then we started looking at each other and talking about the different ways people perceive the world. It was not a matter of judging that one person's perception was better than another's so much as an attempt to observe and recreate the quality and individuality of other people's experience.

With older children it is possible to pursue the observations further and record them in writing. It is possible, for example, to ask students to walk into a room and ask them to observe the room closely and then try to determine the kind of person or family that lives in the place. Another interesting area for observation is the playground. How do different children approach games; who avoids playing and who plunges in? What happens between people, or at least what can you learn from simply watching and trying to project yourself into another's world?

In addition to trying to recreate other worlds, it is possible to experiment with looking at the same phenomenon in many different ways. This can be done physically simply by spending an hour on the floor, an hour on a ladder, and an hour sitting in a chair. A class can be observed from the front of the room, from the back, or from right in the middle. An activity can be observed from a distance or from close in. It can be studied by listening to other people's descriptions of it.

Looking is not always neutral. We often see what we want to see, and one of the benefits of observations that are consciously shifted is that we can uncover our own prejudices as well as learn how others see us. When observing a phenomenon I have found it useful to ask myself the following questions:

> What do I ask of the phenomenon?
> What do I try to tease out of it?
> What do I expect from it?
> What do I wish from it?
> What about it feels comfortable?
> What about it feels uncomfortable?
> What do I like about it?
> What do I dislike about it?

It is easiest to start by observing animals and asking these questions and training one's way of looking. But the human implications are most important. There is so much racial and sexual and class intolerance in our society that we have to begin to undo an unlooking way of living with others. I have done a few sessions with elementary school students who were attending recently desegregated schools and found the children unable to look at each other, even on the simple level of exchanging a glance. As a way of getting them to look at each other fully as people, I began with animals and with a discussion of looking. Eventually they began to look at each other and themselves, to exchange their perceptions of the world and learn from each other.

From there they can move into exploring and changing their own environments, i.e., into the practice of ecological sanity. The original meaning of the word "ecology" hints at how the subject can be approached with young people. The root of the word is "eco," which has its origins in the Greek *oikos,* meaning house or household. "Logy," which comes from the Greek *logos,* means word or wisdom about some subject. Ecology, then, is wisdom about the household. Recently the word "ecology" has come to be extended to refer to the whole environment in which life exists. In this sense, ecology is the wisdom we can master about the earth household; it is a consideration of the whole earth as a house which we must care for since it is our place of dwelling.

We have not been very wise with respect to the care of our earth household. Humans produced more than they consumed and accumulated waste products that poison the environment and may eventually destroy life.

The classroom is an ideal place for the young to begin to learn about the care of the environment. It is possible to study ecology in a formal way. It is also possible to live it.

One way to begin is to survey the waste that accumulates in the classroom during the course of a day or week and see how much of it can be used instead of dumped. In the classroom there are usually a number of organic waste products such as chewing gum, candy, banana peels, apple rinds, and bread crumbs. These products are usually dumped into the same can as nonorganic wastes like paper, old pencils, plastic pens, used notebooks, and so on. Yet these two categories of waste products cannot be disposed of in the same way. The organic waste, in fact, can be used very profitably if one has a small gardening plot in the school, for it can be used to create a compost heap that will develop fertilizer for the garden. In fact, two wastebaskets—one marked "organic" and one "nonorganic"—can be the beginning of wise housekeeping in the classroom.

There is a lot that can be done with nonorganic waste. Old papers can be used to make papier mâché or worked into collages and paintings. They can be used as note scraps, as towels, as wrappings for packages. Pencil stubs can be broken apart and the wood used in small constructions while the lead can be accumulated and used in mechanical pencils. The parts of plastic pens can also be used in many ways. The springs can be used for scientific experimentation, the cartridges for collages and constructions that can decorate the room. I have seen, for example, a wall constructed out of old ball-point pens glued together. The wall is constantly added to as new waste develops and is very functional in the classroom as a divider to make private spaces.

One need not confine the class to studying ways of using waste products in the classroom alone. In our school we have a class in automotive mechanics. The class has spent a lot of time going to junkyards and empty lots where the students have found old engines and carburetors and gear boxes. They have learned to make discarded parts clean and functional. They have also learned how to make their own tools out of discarded scraps of metal and wood. With a soldering iron, a hack saw, and a few other tools, students can make hammers, screwdrivers, drills, and so forth. In this way, they can see the transformation of waste products into useful objects.

There are a lot of other wastes that can be collected and reused in the schools. Old clothes can be used for costumes, or remade into new clothes. Advertisements, old posters, and discarded billboard sections make wonderful reading material and decorations. Last year I found a "sign graveyard" near our school. A large lot was filled with old signs. There were ten-foot-tall letters, large soda bottles and such. We asked for some of the signs for our school and were given them. The letters and figures were worked into a fantasy playground. Other letters and figures were taken apart and the wood and metal were used for other purposes.

We found that mattress factories have more scraps than they

can sensibly dispose of, and so we used them to stuff pillows and cushions, to make stuffed animals, and to weave large tapestries.

In a modest way students can help to develop ways of managing our earth household more wisely. They can be told about the interrelationships of various forms of life and can study life systems. But they can also begin to act upon their own to waste less and want less. They can use their ingenuity in developing new uses for old things and find ways of making our environment less cluttered. Perhaps they can even influence their parents to care more about the way in which they use or discard objects.

BASIC SKILLS *

Teachers should be prepared to teach basic reading, writing, and math, no matter what age youngster they work with or subject they teach. This is not as complex as it might sound. If possible, take a class on diagnosing reading problems or on remedial reading techniques. There are also books such as my *Reading, How to* which provide the information needed to assess students' reading skills and develop a program to help them. Problems with reading often generalize to the rest of the curriculum, especially since reading is a tool needed to read textbooks, lab instructions, novels, poems. Many students who have reading problems are ashamed of the fact and feel that they must be stupid even if they've only been badly taught. To send such a student to a remedial teacher or put them through an elaborate series of formal diagnostic tests is to compound the problems and often alienate the students. However, a reading program can grow out of any area— shop, physical education, science, cooking, art. Beginning with a few phonic variations, moving from reading back to the content of the course, substituting conversation for textbook reading, all lead the student to reading. At the same time one does not have to abandon the subject itself.

---

* It is unfortunate that "basic skills" means solely reading, writing and math in our schools. There are many other basic skills such as cultural awareness, information finding, the ability to teach oneself. It is important to keep in mind that reading and writing do not guarantee intelligence, sensitivity, or compassion.

I know a high school chemistry teacher who teaches complicated chemistry to a group of poor readers. Everything in her lab is
labeled. All the experiments are illustrated with cartoons. Instead
of the regular text, she gives demonstrations and puts summaries
on the chalk board for the students to copy and illustrate. During
the lab period she goes around the room, helping the students with
their experiments and giving five-minute phonic lessons. The
students, not surprisingly, do well in chemistry and reading.
Another teacher I know does the same thing in a junior high school
shop.

However, most people identify the teaching of basic skills with
traditional structured and coercive learning programs. For example, several Septembers ago I mentioned to another teacher that,
"This year I intend to put a heavy emphasis on basic skills." My
coworker said he was glad to see that I had finally come around
and realized that children need structure in order to learn and that
traditional drill and basal readers weren't bad after all. There was
no time to respond, and the conversation ended on an awkward
note, since the children were arriving and we both had to be back
in our classrooms. Like most things in school, there simply was no
time to explore the issues and see them through to a resolution.

However, I have been thinking a lot about what we said to each
other. It is important to keep two things straight—what you want to
achieve and how you intend to get there. Much of the debate over
basic skills confuses these things. The other teacher and I agreed on
goals. We both believed that our students should learn to read and
write and be competent in arithmetic. Because we agreed on this,
we assumed that we must also agree on methods and educational
philosophy.

Goals do not imply methods, nor do they lock one into a single
philosophy. I do not see the need to use basal readers, and I believe
that drill and the teaching of the rules of usage can be confusing
and can actually interfere with learning. I also believe that learning
does not occur through the mastery of small developmentally
sequenced skills in a step-by-step way, but rather occurs through
insight and understanding—different skills and bits of information
falling into place. This occurs in different ways for different people,
and much of what is taught in developmental programs is acquired
through this more global process of understanding.

For me the process of learning to read in a classroom should be continuous with the informal ways in which children are exposed to print all around them, even before they come to school. Children in our society are surrounded by words. When they get up in the morning, they wash with a bar of soap that has a brand name inscribed on it; they brush their teeth with toothpaste that announces its manuiacturer. At breakfast their parents drink a certain brand of coffee; they eat a favorite type of cereal. Just this morning my children had a mixture of Cheerios, Grape Nuts Flakes and Raisin Bran, and my four-year-old knows which cereal comes in which box. With all its cans and boxes and packages and bottles, the kitchen is a veritable reading lab. The same is true for TV and, in urban settings, the street, rife with billboards, signs, and graffiti.

Children are exposed to an enormous amount of print outside of school and play an active role themselves in trying to figure it out. They develop fairly large sight vocabularies and manage to pick up a smattering of phonics (coffee and candy start with a *c;* men's and milk start with an *m* sound). One of the problems children face in school is that this exposure, as well as their personal efforts to understand print, has little or no relationship to what is called "learning to read." Many reading programs assume that children bring no knowledge with them to school.

From my perspective one of the main roles of the teacher is to understand what his or her students know outside of school and to connect this knowledge and experience with what goes on in the classroom. School should be an extension of the rest of one's life and not an instrument of alienation. The classroom can be set up and the reading program designed so that students can draw on their own experiences and take advantage of strengths already developed.

First, teachers must know something about their students' lives. One way is to spend some mornings together having breakfast at the homes of several of your students and then accompanying them to school. For some teachers an afternoon and evening are better. In either case, the point is for you to note all the words and forms of writing they encounter in the course of a day.

If your schedule does not allow for such a plan, you will have to rely upon an imaginative reconstruction of the lives of your students as well as upon what they tell you about what they see and do, what foods they eat, and the other products they consume. The least you can do, however, is take a "word walk" around the school neighborhood and the students' neighborhoods as well, if the two are not the same.

From this information you can begin to design a print environment in which the students feel knowledgeable and strong. On a primary school level, it is sensible to start with the most easily recognized words—labels and boxes and cans and street signs. Coca-Cola, Wheaties, Sanka, and Café Bustelo might all be part of that early sight vocabulary, depending on the community you work in.

Two years ago in my kindergarten/first-grade class, I covered a bulletin board with boxes and packages and labels and made one of our first reading activities Read-A-Box Time. We looked at the boxes, read the labels, talked about the contents and their health value. Nutrition, the development of oral language, as well as sight vocabulary and a knowledge of the sounds of initial consonants, went hand in hand and started from words that were familiar to the students.

I also made up a set of flash cards using all the product names. On one card was a label from a box or can. On another card I wrote the word from the label. Many of the students could identify Coca-Cola when written in the form found on the bottle, but couldn't recognize it when simply printed.

One of the games the students played was matching a word printed on a label with the same word written out. This was done to help the students become flexible in understanding the variety of print faces and be able to read words as words and not solely as pictures. There were a number of other games we played with the cards, ranging from simple read-a-card games to making up stories with the cards and developing shopping lists and estimating how much it costs to buy a bag of groceries.

The room was also filled with signs, such as Beware of Dog, Apartment for Rent, Trespassers Will Be Eaten, Open, Closed, Stop, Exit, Dead End, and one of the students' favorites—No Eating, No Swimming, No Bikes, No Pets, No Picnicking Allowed. If nothing else, all the children quickly learned how to read and spell "no" after looking at the sign a few times. The sign itself led to several interesting discussions of why things were prohibited, what sensible prohibitions were and why people sometimes said "no" just for the sake of it. Again, reading, life outside of school, talking, and phonic skills were integrated.

For older children, and often for the younger ones as well, there is a wealth of material one can use—car ads, menus, bus schedules, newspaper ads, handbills, comic books, airline schedules, travel brochures, signs and ads from local stores, price tags, loan agreements, lease forms, tax forms, ADC and food stamp applications, food stamps, bills, parking tickets, stereo ads, mail order catalogues, programs and scorecards from sports events, local newspapers, concert posters and tickets, record handouts promoting the latest rock or soul or gospel group. Reading at any age connects with life outside of school.

This doesn't mean that all one does in a reading program is use popular culture. Reading can assist young people in moving beyond the immediate into exploring otherwise inaccessible aspects of human experience. A wide assortment of books of all types and on all levels of complexity—including basal readers—are worth having in the classroom. Students can choose to use them or not. *Hooked on Books* by Daniel Fader and Elton McNeil (New York: Putnam, 1968) describes many ways in which paperbacks can be used in the classroom.

Just as a variety of books can be used rather than a single reader, student writing can go far beyond worksheet drill. Writing is an act of inner exploration, a discovery of one's own voice and a process of finding out and saying just what one believes and thinks. I try to have my students do a piece of writing each day—a story, a thought, a short poem, or a description—something in their own voice so that they will learn to write as easily as they learn to read.

I believe that every class could have a writing program which encourages students to write as they talk—naturally, with energy, and with the freedom to make errors and speak in their own voices. I also feel that in order for a program of this sort to develop, the teacher as well as the students has to write and expose his or her writing to the students as much as they expose their work to the teacher. It should be like a conversation where the issue of grades is not present.

There are a number of ways to institute a writing program. With very young children the simplest way is to compose collective stories with the class and ask them to illustrate and copy the stories. For example, one can begin:

One day a wild . . .

I was crying because . . .

I found it more fun to ask the children to begin the stories themselves and take turns finishing. There is always someone who has a story in mind, and I put on the board what the children say as they say it. Sometimes this leads to trouble. For example, one of the students in my class last year always liked to tell stories that involved "dookie" (every child has his or her own favorite word for feces). The stories would go something like this:

> There was a space ship. It got to the moon. The astronaut stepped out on the moon. And he stepped into dookie.

Or the story would read:

> Once there was a diver. He found a treasure chest. He opened the chest and put in his hand. And grabbed a lot of dookie.

All the children loved the dookie stories, but no other kind of stories got told for a while, so I made a rule, the closest to censorship I wanted to get: one dookie story a week. From that time we got a range of stories and still kept the dookie element satisfied.

It is important with really young children to remember how much they can physically write. A story of a few sentences at the beginning of the first grade makes more sense than one of seven or eight lines, which the students could certainly compose but not write.

Collective writing is only one way to have daily writing. Another way is to have a range of writing possibilities available to the class and during a certain time let the students choose how they want to write for that day. Here are a number of possibilities:

a) Diary writing.

b) Collective writing with a small group of friends. Three or four students who pool their language abilities can stretch out much farther than some individuals. There is nothing wrong with encouraging small groups to write one book together, or to get together and help each other write their own books. There is no such thing as cheating in this context—if one person knows how to spell a word or has a good idea about how to end or illustrate a story, it should be shared to everyone's benefit.

c) Bound and stapled books. It pays to make little books for students to fill up and to have crayons and magic markers and pencils and stencils around. Students will quickly figure out ways to make their own books and fill up space. They just need to know that you will give them all the words they don't know. I've spent hours simply standing at the chalk board and writing down words students asked me for while they were writing their books.

d) A box of starters is helpful for students who don't seem to know how to get started. In the box can be a number of starting themes, some interesting pictures, cutouts of comic book characters, samples of books written by other students.

e) A comic book-making center with blank comic books, some commercial comic books, and a sample of the kinds of balloons and marginal comments that are usually used in comics.

You may have noticed that all of this material is teacher-prepared. There is no need for commercially packaged materials to develop a daily writing program. There are some useful resources, such as the *Whole Word Catalogue,* Philip Lopate's *Being with Children* (Garden City, N.Y.: Doubleday, 1975), and Kenneth Koch's *Wishes, Lies, and Dreams* (New York: Chelsea House, 1970). But the most useful material will be that produced by you and your students. It makes sense to provide time for the children to read each other's work and for you to read your work to the class.

Once the idea that it is fine to write begins to develop, it is time to introduce the notion of rewriting. I usually ask my students to pick out the work of theirs they like best and tell them that in order to prepare it for print it is necessary to re-read it, make any changes that would make the work more interesting, and then take care of spelling and punctuation so that other people can read what they have written. It is best to introduce rewriting in the context of publishing. A class literary magazine, a newspaper, a series of poetry broadsides, or school lunch menus composed by the class provide a meaning for rewriting and corrections.

Another good idea is to develop a class library of books written by your students. If you can find a way to type some of their works, there are many handsome ways to bind them into books that can become part of your library program. Your students could even write their own readers. Pauline Johnson's *Creative Bookbinding* is full of ideas on how to bind books simply and elegantly.

Not all corrections need be done for publication, however. I ask my students every week to pick out their favorite piece of writing, and we go over it together. I don't grade the work—just make suggestions for revisions and look at the final copy to see how well it has been presented for another person to read. It is important to understand that standardized spelling is a recent invention and that the prime purpose of correction is to make a work readable by others, and that the prime purpose of rewriting is to enable the author to express himself or herself as accurately and beautifully as possible.

Just as correcting students' work requires judgment and selectivity, so does the use of phonics in a reading program. For some students a bit of judicious and well-selected drill or phonics is called for. My principle is to use no more drill or formal teaching of phonics than is absolutely essential for an individual child. Sometimes someone will stumble over a sound or not understand a particular aspect of reading, e.g., the way *th* sounds at the beginning of a word or the way *ou* functions. Then it is up to the teacher to explain the principle involved and to give the student an opportunity to practice that skill.

Worksheets can be useful, and I especially like to make them up on the spot to meet specific needs. They should not, however, be used to fill up the time in a school day and keep children busy and quiet. I fall into the trap every once in a while and shove a workbook in front of a student who seems restless and about to get out of hand. Now at times like that I use other activities that involve the child and do not attach a negative association to learning, such as suggesting that a student work on a jigsaw puzzle, write a story, make up a comic book, or play a game.

The hardest thing for teachers who begin to use informal reading materials, books, and student writing as the substance of their reading programs is that it will not be possible to measure in traditional terms where every child is at every moment. The way to get around this is to set up your program so that you will be able to sit and read with each child at least once a week. Even though you won't know which color workbook they are in or at which level on the behavioral objective scale they fall, you will know a much more important thing—how well they are reading.

The same remarks hold true for math, though it is harder for teachers to develop their own math curriculum unless they feel comfortable with the subject. It is advisable to take a few math classes if you are uneasy with the subject. With a bit of ease it is possible to learn what informal math one's students know, to discover what games they play, how they deal with money, with dividing things up among themselves, with measuring food and the sizes of clothes and shoes. From this informal knowledge it is possible to move toward more abstract math, to make up systems with one's students or study traditional ones. Sometimes it is even sensible to introduce a concept in mathematics by creating a system. Once I tried to introduce the concepts of length and systems of measurement that way.

A few years ago in my class I showed the students a simple visual illusion and asked them whether the lines were the same or different sizes. One line looked longer than the other though they were both the same size, which one of the students guessed. I asked her to prove it to me. She laid a piece of paper along both of the lines, marking the beginning and the end of the lines and showed me that they coincided. She proved they were the same size by indirect comparison. I explained at that point that there were other ways to measure things and asked one of the boys to trace his hand a number of times. Then by cutting out and taping the hands together I made a "Ben's-hand ruler," and asked the class how many Ben's hands long one of the tables in the room was. Ben reserved for himself the privilege of making that first measurement. All of the students wanted to make their own measuring systems, and so Tonia's hands and Charlie's feet and Celine's shoes all gave rise to standard measures. We had a proliferation of systems, which created confusion and brought the class to see the need for standardization of measures. Carol's hand was chosen by lot to be the standard for our class's system.

I raised a new problem. How could you measure the size of a pack of matches or a stick of gum in terms of Carol's hand, which was bigger than either of them? The need to break down the measure became obvious, and someone suggested that we use the length of Carol's thumb from the tip of the nail to the first joint as a smaller measure in our system. It worked out elegantly since five of these units made up one Carol's hand. We had the beginning of a system of measurement with simple relationships between its parts.

In order to measure the length of our room a larger measurement was needed, and so we decided to call ten Carol's hands a table since that was just about the length of the tables in the room. Later the students developed a hundred-hand measure, called a room, and made a two-room tape measure so that we could measure the playground and measure out ballfields and determine the length of paper airplane and glider flights. Thus, our system, which started from scratch, evolved into the following form:

Standard measure: Carol's hand as traced December 7, 1973
Equivalences: 5 thumbs equal 1 hand
 10 hands equal 1 table
 10 tables or 100 hands equal 1 room

At this point I brought in some rulers that had both the metric and imperial systems on them. I explained that there were two basic systems used in the world to measure length these days and that soon, as people traded with each other and became more dependent upon communicating with each other, there will be one system, the metric system, which seems the easiest to deal with. The students, who were first-graders, had no trouble using the ruler with inches or with centimeters; they adapted to thinking in two systems without trouble. Also they understood the reason why more than one system had evolved because they had started from scratch and could understand how other people developing systems of measurement could develop a variety of different systems. They could see something as basic as the creation of measures as the creative act of real people and not as an abstract, universal, and unquestioned principle.

It is possible to build all kinds of systems from scratch in math. For example, it is possible to invent numerical symbols, to try to add and subtract using only two or three symbols without even mentioning the notion of systems of different bases. I have found that ideas flow more freely and understanding develops when invention precedes exposure to already developed systems.

This is only a small example of what can be done. Fortunately, there are a number of excellent books that lay out the development of a student-centered mathematics curriculum from kindergarten through senior high school. For elementary school, the Nuffield Mathematics Series (New York: John Wiley and Sons,) provides a rich source of curriculum ideas and ways to teach the basic skills of measuring, calculating, and problem solving.

The Cuisenaire Company of America also carries a number of excellent books on the teaching of mathematics to young children. I've found *Mathematics and the Child* by Frederique Papy and *Graphs and the Child* by Papy and Frederique particularly useful. A free catalogue listing these and other books and materials on mathematics is available from the Cuisenaire Company of America, 12 Church Street, New Rochelle, New York 10805.

On a secondary level and for young but precocious mathematicians I've found the following books to be excellent: *Mathematics; a Human Endeavor: A Textbook for Those Who Think They Don't Like the Subject,* Harold R. Jacobs (San Francisco: W.H. Freeman, 1970); *Modern Mathematics and the Teacher,* Lucienne Felix (Cambridge: Cambridge University Press, 1966) and *Playing with Infinity* by Rozsa Peter (New York: Atheneum, 1964).

OBSERVING AND LISTENING

Observing and listening to one's students are skills that develop through experience and require judgment as well as an understanding of the broader contexts students live in. It is not enough to look and hear. Imagine the following:

It is after lunch. Two students walk into the room cursing each other. One is big, popular, known to be very easygoing, but able to defend herself when necessary. The other is small and slight, withdrawn in class, though very pleasant to talk to when the other students are not around. During class hours they have nothing to do with each other.

They look at you and suddenly become silent. The more outgoing student goes over to some of her friends and they gossip a bit, pick up some books, and read together. The other student sits staring at a wall, her fists clenched. When you turn to talk to her, she is as pleasant and compliant as always. By three o'clock everything seems forgotten. However, as soon as the class is dismissed, the two students begin to curse each other again and prepare to fight. Before anything actually develops, the two are separated by other students and leave the school. The next day you prepare for a fight, but the two girls come to school together, arms around each other as if they are the best of friends.

What to make of what you observed? Of course, there is no single interpretation, and no full understanding of events like this can ever be gained merely by knowing what goes on in the classroom. However, certain things can be guessed at on the basis of how the girls behave. No single instance is enough to give a picture of a person's feelings and motives, and teachers should avoid making quick judgments about their students. For example, it is clear that the shy, withdrawn girl is willing to stand up for herself and has internal strength that may not be apparent in the classroom. The more outgoing student also has a great deal of self-discipline, or she would not have calmed down on seeing the teacher. Both girls let themselves be separated by other students, indicating that face may have been involved more than anger. The fact that they seemed friendly the next day indicates that some sort of testing occurred and that since a face-saving draw took place (neither had to back down; their friends helped them out of the situation), they could be equals and therefore friends. One did not become a gloating master, nor the other a plotting slave.

A final thing should be mentioned. The students as a group acted as a strong mediating force. They knew how to act collectively. Often this strength is never allowed to develop in the classroom, and teachers never know it exists.

In drawing these conclusions, the emphasis has been on the students, both as a group and as individuals. To observe these strengths, however, the teacher has to feel unthreatened. If cursing seemed threatening, if the difference between threat, play, and actual violence was blurred, the teacher's observations would be more a function of his or her own fear than the students' behavior.

A recent visitor to my class who walked in on a fight between two boys was horrified by what he saw as my indifference to the physical safety of one of the children. The boys—one black and one white—were the same size and age. They had been eyeing each other for a few days, testing to see who would become dominant. That morning one boy shoved the other, and the two squared off. At that point the visitor arrived. Both boys were swinging more at the air than at one another. For about thirty seconds I stayed back and let them go at each other before moving in to break up the fight. Neither boy had established dominance, and I could sense a mutual respect developing that would be good for them and for the communal spirit in the class during the rest of the year.

My guest saw things differently, however. "Why did you let that black kid pick on that white kid?" he asked. That's the way he had seen the fight. Because a black and a white boy were fighting, he immediately assumed that the black child started it.

That wasn't the only problem. My visitor asked me why I hadn't stopped the fight or, after breaking up the battle, hadn't even lectured the students about the evils of fighting in general, implying that my attitude would encourage fighting in the future.

I tried to explain my feelings about fighting in the classroom. It is often impossible to pinpoint the reason for a fight. Sometimes it is hostility brought into the classroom from the street, which the teacher just doesn't know about. Other times it is the need of students to establish a pecking order in their own ranks or to respond to a real or imagined insult. Occasionally, it is simply play-acting. In its worst and most intolerant form it is bullying or brutalizing of certain individuals by others.

I refuse to tolerate this last form of violence and deal with it by protecting the victim and controlling the oppressor, while also trying to deal with the oppressor's need to hurt and the victim's passivity when attacked. However, when students push each other, feel each other out, wrestle in a friendly way, tell people to leave them alone and otherwise defend their work, their space, and their integrity, I let things go to the point at which people might get hurt.

In a classroom where students are free to relate to each other in informal ways, testing out is inevitable. A congenial and comfortable atmosphere can result only from human experimentation—

from the students finding out about one another and learning not to fear each other and to defend themselves.

This doesn't mean that I encourage fighting among children, but that I do not view it in moral terms. If two students fight, that does not mean that one is bad and the other is good, or that one started it and has to be punished. Both might have been, for example, pushed into a difficult situation by friends.

As there is an increase in the comfort students feel with each other and in their involvement with work, there is a decrease in fighting. As fewer skirmishes are turned into major disciplinary problems, fewer squabbles will develop into serious fights.

I have found that in classes where physical contact between students is prohibited and punished severely, fights, when they do develop, are serious and dangerous. In more accepting and physical environments, where casual physical contact and playful fighting are not considered evil, hostility is less likely to build.

When I see a real fight developing, I simply break it up before it gets serious and tell the participants to do something more productive. My emphasis is on what else could be done, on other ways of talking or relating to each other, and not at all on punishing the act itself.

This causes problems for people like my visitor who have inarticulated racist views and always assume that it is the black child who starts a fight or gets physical. Teachers may have other unexpressed expectations related to violence that they must recognize in themselves. For example, do not always assume that larger children start fights; neither should you assume that girls do not resort to physical violence. Each fight is a particular instance of how two or a number of people choose to relate to each other. All fights should not be lumped into a single category as if they represented one type of behavior.

As a last comment, I believe it is important for all people to learn how to defend themselves and not live in fear. At the same time, it is important that they not depend on violence or use it as the only way they can reach other people ̀or test their intentions. Children have to be helped to overcome their fears of each other, especially when they are of different economic, racial, and cultural backgrounds.

Children have to meet one another physically and casually as well as in controlled learning situations. They have to be trusted to get acquainted and to take care of themselves as much as possible. While it is a teacher's job to set limits on physical contact and to prevent anyone from getting hurt, the teacher has to learn to distinguish dangerous confrontations from situations in which students learn how to defend themselves and how not to be afraid of the world. A teacher worries whether the students will learn how to read, but the children worry more about whether they will be liked and be able to live in school free from fear or the need to act tough. Both of these faces of the same discomfort have to be worked out—and they will be—as long as physical contact is not equated with evil behavior of murderous intent.

It always helps to talk to students before or after class, to know something of the community, to observe students on the playground, and most of all to withhold moral judgment until you have seen and heard a lot and feel confident that you understand what you have experienced.

Here is another example of how teachers must observe and listen to their students. One of the boys in your class acts crazy whenever you ask him to read. He says the book is boring, reading is irrelevant to his life. He calls you a fascist pig for trying to force him to read and says he just wants to be left alone. During your reading lessons he sits quietly, looking bored, though there is the outside possibility that he might be listening and not wanting you to know. If you just observe him during reading time, it would seem that he's slow or for some reason unable to learn. However, the other students look to him as the greatest source of sports information in the class. He also knows what's playing at all the local movies, who's at what club, what the top twenty records are. Some of this involves reading, all of it involves being aware of a world outside the school that is of value to the other students, though irrelevant for their school experience.

The knowledge of this person can be brought to the center of the curriculum. What he knows and the other students value can become a vehicle for them to educate the teachers, who can then use this material to help the students with reading and writing. Or it can become a barrier. Then that student's defiance cannot be overcome or turned to strength within the school because the rewards he gets from the other students for standing up for what they value are much greater than those a mere teacher can offer.

Students have many reasons for avoiding reading or other academic studies. Some have been humiliated so much in school that they would rather be considered dumb than expose themselves to failure. Others have been convinced they are dumb and act the part. There are students who are bored and angered by what they are made to read. Some students need to move around or listen to music in order to concentrate. It is the teacher's responsibility to listen, observe, understand, and then work with the students to build a congenial learning place where diverse needs and styles are accommodated and welcomed.

Listening has another dimension. Often students ask for resources and express the desire to learn things that are not in the curriculum or that their teacher is not competent to deal with. Requests for knowledge and skills should not be denied, no matter how much they might put you out. If someone wants to learn about airplanes, sharks, volcanoes, sex, embryos, police, weapons, self-defense, TV, then chase up some information or resources, or learn with the students. I have found that following up on one student's request to learn something of special interest to him or her opens up the rest of the students; it tells them you will listen to them and take their interests seriously, too. Then you as a teacher can become a personal resource to your students, someone who will find a way to help them learn what they care to know, not as a favor because they are good or obedient, but because it is your job.

Notes are a valuable aid to observation. It helps to begin the school year with a notebook that has four or five blank pages for each student in the class (this book would be in addition to any notes you made on curriculum or tentative lesson plans). Then, as you begin to notice things about the students, learn their names, interests, and social roles in the class, you can record these observations. If you re-read the notes every two weeks or so, you might learn a lot. For example, one student might have no entries for the first few weeks, indicating that he or she might be neglected or at least not known to you. In other cases, change can be detected that you might not be able to perceive because it occurred slowly over a long period of time. It also makes sense to record your gut feelings about the students since these feelings will certainly affect how to treat them and might account for how they react to you. This notebook is probably best kept private or, at most, shared with people you trust.

Here is a condensed sample of some notes I kept several years ago:

Student: Martin, age 8 years
September notes:
1. Martin is very pleasant, a bit of an urchin, thin, blond, pretend tough, hangs around me a lot.
2. I think Martin tried to hit Johnny with a hammer when I wasn't watching—I'm not sure—something makes me uneasy about him.
3. Today I'm sure. Tom [the student teacher] had to grab the hammer away from him.

October:
1. Martin can't read, spell, do anything but aggress.
2. He makes me nervous, I've taken to watching him all the time, it's become exhausting and boring.

November:
1. Should we get rid of Martin; I hate to feel defeated but he's making me angry.
2. Today Todd bumped into Martin and he exploded—started biting and kicking and scratching Todd at the same time he was crying like a baby himself. I had to hold him tight.
3. Tried to explain to him that Todd bumped him by accident. He couldn't accept it. Same thing happened today with Elizabeth and Martin. He doesn't think anything happens accidentally.

December:
1. Hope I can hold on with Martin until Christmas. He's still hard to reach but hangs around the other kids a lot more—as if he doesn't know how to get involved with them.
2. Another bump—another fight. I blew up at Martin, he began crying, said no one liked him, he couldn't do anything. He ran out of the room. I waited until after 3 and talked to him. Told him the way to make friends was ask people to play with him. *He said nobody liked him.* I asked him who he liked and he said Matthew. We agreed that he would ask Matthew to play with him tomorrow.

3. It worked—for about 20 minutes and then the usual bump and fight. We agreed to try it again tomorrow.*

SETTING LIMITS

There are certain rules of behavior that have to be enforced in the classroom for the sake of group survival. I have found the following sufficient:

1. No person (student, teacher, or other adult) is to be allowed to injure or bully another.
2. No person is to be allowed to kill or maim himself.
3. No one is to be allowed to interfere with or prevent others from working.
4. No one is to be allowed to destroy any student's work or classroom material.

These four rules set clear limits of acceptable behavior. Within them there is a wide range of freedom that can develop. If anything, these rules protect the freedom of individuals within the context of a group rather than restrict it. Enforcing these rules can be the responsibility of the teacher, though ideally they should be maintained by the group as a whole.

I explain these rules to my students during the first week of school in as positive a way as possible. One year I made the mistake of beginning with these prohibitions rather than showing the students what they could do first. Some students became hostile the first day, almost by reflex. I said "you can't"—their bodies responded "I will." These rules became challenges to battle, rather than accepted conditions for mutual survival. It took several weeks to overcome that negative note. Since then I introduce the students to the possibilities offered in the class—to the activity centers, to what I know, to different games and materials. Then I explain the rules as conditions necessary to allow things to be done.

---

* Martin stayed in my class for two years. It took a full year to calm him down. During the second year he was a proud senior member of the class and he was able to catch up with other youngsters his age. He is also delightfully strong and defiant, a challenging student.

There is always a testing period, and new teachers can find this the most trying time of their first year in the classroom. Some student will punch another, or deliberately break a test tube, or rip up another student's drawing. At that point, all the students will watch the teacher to discover how he or she deals with the rules. Fights are easiest to deal with. Simply stop them, separate the combatants, and have them stay still until they are ready to do something more productive in the room. If the combatants refuse to cool down, one has to be removed from the room, by force if necessary. What is crucial is that once the fight is over, you drop it. Don't turn two students who happen to fight once in a while into "bad pupils" and expect that because they fought they'll do everything else wrong.

Breaking equipment or destroying work is cause for anger, which a teacher should not be afraid to express. Let everyone know how you feel, perhaps separate the offender for a while. Again, don't turn him into an incorrigible criminal, but don't turn your back either.

A teacher must respond consistently to whatever limits he or she decides are necessary in the classroom, or chaos and continued defiance will likely result. Often students will complain about the teacher's stopping fights or being angry with destructive behavior. My response to being called "bossy" or dictatorial is to tell the students that they are free to enforce the rules themselves or live together harmoniously so that the rules won't need enforcement. Little by little, the testing eases up. Students assume responsibility for each other's behavior and work as they get involved in learning and creating things. The more the students enjoy and value what they are doing, the more they will fight to see it is not destroyed. In a boring situation, so-called discipline problems are inevitable since the struggle for power and control is then more interesting than the content of what is supposed to be learned.

With a bit of experience observing students, a teacher can come to anticipate fights or destructive acts before they develop. Some teachers seem to have antennae that respond to glance, tone, set of body. They can then prevent destructive things from happening by a private word, a look, a gesture. Often students are destructive in order to command an adult's undivided attention. Acknowledging this need and giving your undivided attention to those students at other moments often eliminates the need to act defiantly.

I have found that private games often develop with students whose behavior you can anticipate. Once I caught a boy about to drop our class microscope. I raised my eyebrows in mock horror. He smiled embarrassedly and put the microscope back on the table. The next day he picked up a hammer, waited until I saw him, and then went over to a papier-mâché horse and pretended he was going to smash it. I made the same face, and he smiled, not from embarrassment, but because I got his point and joined in the joke. We played the game for a few weeks and began to talk for the first time in the year.

In an open and happy learning situation everyone will try his or her hand at defiance or testing the limits once in a while. This is a healthy way young people have of testing their power against the power of adults. So long as no serious damage can result, I try to enforce the limits, at the same time letting the students know I respect their strength. It's a matter of giving a bit, of talking about what's happening, of you and your students being moral equals.

Moral equality can be threatening to adults, for it implies that the same rules apply to you as to your students. You cannot hurt or bully them, destroy their work, interfere with them when they are working. If you give them the opportunity, your students will let you know when you are making their lives intolerable or uncomfortable. You have to learn how to listen to these criticisms and, if they are well-founded, change your own behavior. A teacher cannot expect less of himself or herself than of the students.

DEVELOPING THE ENVIRONMENT

Even the most barren classroom has more objects in it than most people are accustomed to organizing and managing. There are class sets of books, pencils, erasers, art supplies, dictionaries, library books, students' record cards, notices, notes. Many beginning teachers feel drowned by the sheer number of things they have to manage and succumb to chaos or become stingy and compulsive about order and cleanliness. There is a line between those painful extremes—it is possible to keep supplies and resources on open shelves and available to students without having everything destroyed or lost. Several things have to be done first. Before school opens, it is important to spend a few days tearing your classroom apart and taking complete inventory of what is available to you. Organize everything so you know where things are and can get them quickly when you need them. Also indulge in an orgy of labeling. Get a DymoMarker or use masking tape and magic markers. Label every shelf and closet. The labels will help you to explain to the students where things belong. They will also help you work your way into the classroom and become familiar with the space. Moving into a new classroom is like moving into a new apartment or house—it takes a while to smell out the space, establish a place of your own, and feel comfortable.

Every day come to school at least a half hour early and set things up. I've found that when games are laid out, books made available, art projects set up, students settle in more quickly. Also that half hour of wandering about the room before the students arrive gives you a chance to think about the previous day, look at or read the students' work, and prepare new material that some students need or ask for. I've found it a bad habit to try to sneak in required paperwork before the students arrive. It always leaves me with a bad taste, as if the day began with the worst aspect of being a teacher, rather than with the most interesting and creative aspects. Paperwork is much better done during lunch or at home over a glass of wine.

With the classroom fairly well set up, it is reasonable to expect students to put away what they use and to clean up their own messes. This will be a hassle at the beginning of the year, but it is always easy to get students to clean up if you pitch in too. The teacher is a worker and has to get his or her hands dirty along with the students, as well as in their service.

A half hour after school is a sensible complement to the half hour before school. The students will never fully clean up unless cleaning replaces learning. There will be many times when three o'clock comes and too much is happening to have the room in order. You just have to become friends with the custodian and push a broom and use a sponge. No matter how tired you are, it is never smart to leave the room in a mess. The mess will face you and the students the next morning and will invite further disorder. It is crucial to take care of the classroom, although not so much that you become the students' slave nor so little that both you and the students come to be disgusted by the place. The balance between cleanliness and openness, the creative disorder and equally creative order that a smoothly functioning classroom has is not a casual thing. It takes extra time to find this balance, especially during the first few years of teaching, yet it is essential to have in order to create a comfortable and congenial place for people to spend five hours a day.

DISCOVERING HIDDEN RESOURCES

Every school has hidden resources. Often administrators try to use as few books and supplies as possible. For some reason it breaks many principals' hearts to see new books soiled by the hands of students, or to see tools used (there might be a lawsuit), or science equipment consumed. However, the books and the supplies are there because they belong to the young people and are paid for by the community. They are not owned by the school, and it is possible to force principals to use them. However, one first has to know what is available. To do this one must have access to the supply closets, the book closets, the basement storerooms, the audio-visual room, and also to the inventory lists in the school. It is not difficult in most schools to find ways to sniff around and take your own personal inventory of what is available. For example, volunteer to take inventories or help with the distribution of books. By volunteering to do what others consider dirty work, it is possible to get the keys to the doors that hide the materials. Another way that I used to gain access to school supplies was to become friendly with the teacher aides, who are usually given the teachers' dirty work to do. Many aides care more about the students and identify with them more closely than teachers, and certainly than administrators, since they live in the community and know the children informally as well as in the classroom. They would like to see the school's resources used and will often take it upon themselves to turn over the materials that the principal wants to hide. They also have all the keys, as do janitors.

It also makes sense to visit the old-time teachers, since they have a tendency to hoard materials and books, and to protect them from the students. Find an overstocked room and put pressure on the teacher to loosen up. If you need help, tell some parents that their children are being cheated, and indicate what some other classrooms have available.

Volunteer to be supervisor of the audio-visual team or the science squad or the office squad. Infiltrate those organizations, and get to know what exists in your school, and make sure it gets used.

Take a trip down to the central distribution warehouse. Look at all of the material that is being discarded as obsolete or auctioned off for almost nothing. See what can be used by your school and demand it. Bring a truck or van with you.

Also, see the new material coming into the district, and make sure your kids get what is due them. There are as many hoarders at the central office as there are at each school.

Get hold of the state and federal guidelines for the allocation of materials to schools. It is possible that your school is entitled to federally or state subsidized material and that your principal or district is too lazy to apply. For example, there is federal money available for the purchase of science supplies which many schools never take advantage of. The more you know about what is due the children, the stronger the position you will be in when you demand it.

Another way to get resources is to offer to share what you have with another teacher. Having a friend on the staff never hurts you, and, if you are willing to pool resources, your students will have that much more material to draw on. Also, two teachers standing together are more than twice as strong as one teacher in opposition. Two teachers and their students (usually between fifty and sixty people) are a minischool, a school within a school, a cell, a powerful unit from which one can begin to organize. They are also a unit that can provide protection so that one can learn to teach well and have something to offer when change becomes possible.

MAKING TRANSITIONS

Teachers have to learn how to provide transitions for their pupils. It is not possible for most young people to make choices after five or six years of being told what to do every minute they are in school. It is equally hard for them to share resources, help other students, or decide what they want to learn after years of being expected to hoard, compete, and conform. Transitional situations often have to be provided. Some students need workbooks for a while; others want to memorize times tables or have weekly spelling tests. Young people are no different from adults. When faced with new possibilities they want something old and predictable to hold onto while risking new freedom. Inexperienced teachers often make the mistake of tearing down the traditional attitudes their students have been conditioned to depend upon before the students have time to develop alternate ways of learning and dealing with school. In their impatience they become cruel to students who do not change fast enough or who resist change altogether. One just cannot legislate compassion or freedom. Teaching as a craft involves understanding how people learn; as an art it involves a sensitive balance between presenting and advocating things you believe and stepping away and encouraging your students to make their own sense of your passion and commitment.

This is no less true with respect to changing sexual stereotypes in the classroom than with helping students overcome their fear of making decisions. Most classrooms are set up so that girls paint and draw, boys play kickball. Girls dress up and play house; boys have fun with trucks and blocks. Girls read; boys enjoy math and science. Girls gossip; boys fight.

All these stereotypes existed in my kindergarten/first-grade class last year. And I didn't have to do anything to encourage such role playing other than have paint, balls, blocks, trucks, and dress-ups available! The boys hung around each other, pretending to be tough. The girls stayed together and acted good.

There were a few exceptions—Barbara was rougher than any of the boys and played with them, while Matthew was extremely artistic and theatrical. He spent lots of time working on art projects with the girls and was the male in their fantasies. Other than these two children, the five- and six-year-olds in my class already subscribed to all the sexual stereotypes of our culture—including the tragic tie of violence to maleness. Even the exceptions were to be expected: one tomboy and one artist.

It proved to be more difficult to undo these roles than to teach reading skills. It was hard to dissuade the boys from violence and get them involved in poetry, art, music, and theatre. I wanted to encourage the girls to be more active and willing to tackle math, science, athletics, and construction activities.

At first the students were reluctant to talk about boy-versus-girl preferences. They simply believed that that's the way things were supposed to be. Finally, through breaking down the boundaries of different subjects, renaming places and activities, and redistributing resources in the room, we created certain conditions that allowed both the girls and boys to step out of their sex-based roles without losing face. Let me describe some of the things that worked.

I started by breaking down the boundaries of different subjects. In the beginning we had an art center, a small cooking area, and a workbench with a few hammers and saws. Art and cooking were the girls' interests; the shop was taken over by the boys. The solution was to integrate the shop, kitchen, and studio, keeping all the tools, such as mixing spoons, measuring cups, rulers, hammers, and paint brushes, in a single place along with the materials we used—nails, paints, wood, paper, fabric, plastic, and so on. As long as there were no clear boundaries established, the girls didn't feel as awkward or seem to have as much trouble handling a hammer or saw. And the boys could paint and imagine they were doing shop work if they needed to. Boys and girls could work side by side and together in groups.

The same kind of breakdown had to take place in the science center. We started the year off by studying electricity and magnetism. There were batteries, bells, buzzers, wire, and magnets available for everyone to experiment with, but the boys monopolized the material no matter how much the student teacher and I tried to intervene. The boys and girls had equally strong reactions to making noise with the bells—reluctance from the girls, delight from the boys. Only after a while, when the boys became bored, did a few girls use the equipment. (The exception was Barbara, of course, who worked with the boys all along.)

The next theme we dealt with was light, which was conceived more broadly by the students, so more joined in the activities. We introduced the concept of light by first playing with mirrors and kaleidoscopes and then trying some sleight-of-hand magic. We considered the eye and how it gets tricked sometimes, which naturally led to making flip books and seeing how motion pictures worked. We moved on to picture taking, producing movies, and eventually even to making an eight-minute animated cartoon. The study of light incorporated science, math (measurement was involved since the students had to decide whether the lines in a visual illusion were actually equal or not), art (we made kaleidoscopes, used mirrors in collages, and constructed light boxes), theater, and technology.

As a whole experience, the theme of light did not lend itself to sex definition. So girls and boys equally handled cameras, made characters and backdrops for the cartoon, dressed up and acted out roles in the movie, learned to use a metric ruler, and so on. The children acted as individuals, not stereotypes.

Another technique I found successful was renaming the centers in the room and some activities. For example, in one corner of the room there was a dollhouse with dress-ups, a wooden stove, refrigerator, and all the traditional paraphernalia. Changing the name to "haunted house," "fantasy house" or "the theater" opened the space up to more children and a wider range of activities. Over the course of a year, the fantasy center became a spaceship, a soul music theater, a restaurant, an apartment house, a stable, a barn, a dance stage, and the place where our superheroes—male and female, black and white—lived and worked.

I also renamed the library corner "the bookmaking center" and stocked it with rubber stamps, staplers, bookbinding materials, stencils, samples of books done by other children, comic books, and magazines, as well as the usual supply of "readers." This encouraged a wider range of activities involving reading and writing, and during the course of the year *all* the students used the center. Previously, the library corner had been monopolized by a few shy girls, who read amazingly well but did little else in class. As the number of activities grew, so did the participation and personalities of these girls.

A third strategy that worked well was the redistribution of many of the resources in the classroom—blocks and toy cars were kept with the dolls, while paints and crayons were put in the bookmaking and science centers. Sometimes simply changing the character of the resources available broadened the use of a particular area. We added fancy men's clothes to the dress-up corner, and the boys started using it. After a while, the children also began experimenting with cross dressing—the boys playing with dresses and the girls with suits and ties. This was always done in a theatrical context, as part of a play or impromptu musical, so it was never a charged issue.

A few other shifts in resources produced interesting results—putting books in the fantasy house, and musical instruments in the science center. Eventually, the students themselves moved things around: they made a boat in the fantasy house and brought checker games there to pass the time while they were at sea, used the bells and buzzers to make a doorbell for the haunted house, built a go-cart and painted it.

All of these developments took place slowly over the course of the year, and the roles never changed completely. There were still times when the boys and girls acted as two distinct groups. However, that became one of *many* modes in which the students functioned, rather than the only one.

With older children changing the environment is less effective in dealing with oppressive stereotypes than redefining the nature of what is studied and even occasionally changing the language.

Some years ago, when I was teaching sixth grade in an all-black elementary school, one of the students walked up to the board and challenged me: "Mr. Kohl, I dare you to read this!" and then he proceeded to write *history*.

I knew there was some trick, but let myself be baited and said the word was history, which meant the study of things that happened in the past. He laughed and said that actually he had put a misspelled word on the board—the word should have read his-story, the story of how the past was supposed to be from the

perspective of the white man. I couldn't disagree, for at the time I
had on my desk a history book which misrepresented the contemporary United States as a peaceful and perfect democracy and
treated the past history of most of the peoples that make up this
nation with scorn and derision. It was as if most of us, Polish and
Jewish and African and Mexican and Irish and Italian, had no
culture before we arrived, or as if those elements of the culture we
arrived with were burdens and signs of inferiority.

More recently, a student asked me the same question. She put
on the board the word "history" and explained that the original
spelling was, indeed, his-story and that women had been left out or
else it would have been called "herstory" or "ourstory."

The notion of "ourstory" fascinated me, and so I decided to
pursue that instead of talking about why people in power used
history to justify their present status, which seemed obvious and a
dead end in terms of learning. So instead I suggested and the class
decided to pursue ourstory—to investigate the past of our community and our own families, and to uncover the reason why our city,
Berkeley, was the way it was in the present.

We decided to do some research in the library, but to
emphasize using people's experiences and recollections as much as
possible. A logical starting point was the families and relatives of
the students in the class. We wanted to ask people questions, gather
old documents such as letters, diaries, pictures, magazines, maps,
toys, and tools. We also wanted to tape people's recollections,
record stories of the old times, learn about the physical appearance
of the community fifty years ago, learn about what old people
thought had changed and what had remained the same.

We spent a few days discussing what things one might learn
most from and wrote up a questionnaire designed to provide
information so we could begin to generate an account of the recent
past in our city. The questionnaire was given by the students to
their relatives and neighbors. It went like this:

> The students in our class are trying to find out about the people in
> Berkeley and about what the city was like before we were born. We
> need your experience to help us. Could you answer these questions
> in writing? If you do not have time, we will be glad to come and tape
> your answers. Thank you.

1. Were you born in Berkeley?
2. If not, why and when did you come here? Do you remember what it was like when you arrived? Do you remember any specific things? Do you have things you brought with you? Do you remember your reasons for leaving the old community?
3. If you were born in Berkeley, what was it like? Where did you grow up? Has the neighborhood changed? What did you do during an ordinary day when you were five? Ten? Fifteen? What was going to school like? What games did you play or dances did you do or songs did you sing as a young person?
4. What is the oldest thing in your possession? Could we see it, and could you tell us about it?
5. What nursery rhymes did your parents and grandparents tell you? What dreams do you remember as a child?
6. Who ran Berkeley when you were young? What did people do for a living? Do you have pictures or other things you've saved from the time you were young?
7. What do you remember of other people you grew up with? Are many of them still around? What were they like, and what are they doing now?
8. Do you remember the oldest people you knew as a child? What were they like, and where did they come from? Do you remember any of their stories or songs?

The students, who were fifth- and sixth-graders, took the questionnaires home, and the response was amazing. It was as if the young people had never asked the old to tell them what they knew or experienced or had to teach. We learned that what is now called Berkeley was once two towns, Berkeley and Ocean View, and that the poorer town, Ocean View, was swallowed by the richer Berkeley. We also learned that Ocean View–Berkeley was a lumber shipping port and that many Finnish people settled in the town to work in lumbering industry. Berkeley was identified with the university, Ocean View with the working people in the town, a split that is still very strong despite the incorporation.

We found the old town hall and fire station of Ocean View. In fact, they were across the street from where one of the students lived, but she did not know about it until her grandmother told her.

We also found out where most of the people in the class came from. There were people from New York, Mississippi, Oklahoma, and Chicago. Many people had different personal reasons for moving west, but a general discontent with the urban North and the rural South emerged as the main reason. People came for a newer, freer life and could tell us of their hopes and disappointments.

One of the other reasons that people came west was the shipbuilding industry developed on the West Coast by Henry Kaiser during the Second World War. After the war, the industry collapsed, leaving many people who had moved from the rural South to find new ways to survive.

As we talked to people in the community, they showed us photos, letters, diaries; they told us tales and reflected on the Second World War, the Depression, upon good and bad times. We had a wealth of material out of which we could piece together ourstory, which, it became clear to the students, was neither one story for all of us nor a simple story for any of us.

We supplemented the materials we had gathered with visits to the public archives and the university library. A number of graduate students were helpful. A picture began to emerge of a diverse community that had many conflicts and divisions. Many things that had seemed so new to the students and myself were just newer forms of old social and political problems that had existed for years.

In class we talked about doing something with all the materials we gathered—of showing the community a portrait of itself. We dreamed about taking one of the parks or a school yard and creating a living museum, utilizing the materials we gathered and the people we talked to. We never did it, but the idea still intrigues me. The plan was to display old photographs, have people teach the games and songs they knew as children, have tapes of old stories and copies of letters and diaries. We also wanted to have different guest speakers from the community talking about their childhood. In addition, we planned to make a giant map and time line of the lives of the people in our class and their relatives. The map was to be a world map and would trace where we all came from, as far back as we could puzzle it out. We wanted to surround the map with pictures we had taken of the people in the community juxtaposed with photos they had shown us of their youth. Our goal was to make the community come alive with a sense of itself, something I feel could probably be attempted in any community in our nation.

There are two groups who managed to realize what we only started. Both are located in Appalachia, and their work is available to be studied as a model for discovering ourhistory. The first group is called Foxfire and is located in Rabun Gap, Georgia. *Foxfire* magazine and the books *Foxfire 1, Foxfire 2,* and *Foxfire 3* (Garden City, N.Y.: Doubleday, 1972; 1973; 1975), which were compiled by Eliot Wigginton and his high school students, document the ways and lore and wisdom of the old folk in southern Appalachia. Eliot Wigginton has also written a book called *Moments* (available from Ideas, 1785 Massachusetts Avenue, N.W., Washington, D.C. 20036) which shows people how to produce their own versions of *Foxfire.* The Appalshop, which is in Whitesburg, Kentucky, has produced a series of marvelous films on the lives and work of poor Appalachians, which does in film what *Foxfire* does in print. If anything, the Appalshop films are more immediate and less romantic; they deal with such things as childbirth, hog killing, religious services, strip mining. These films are available for a modest rental fee from Appalshop, Inc., Box 743, Whitesburg, Kentucky 41858.

CONVINCING PARENTS OF THE VALUE OF ONE'S WORK

One of the problems teachers face is the cautious nature of many parents, who want a traditional classroom for their children and have never been exposed to nontraditional modes of learning. Therefore, parents need to be educated and learn what to expect from open classrooms.

I have seen many potentially sympathetic parents walk into open classrooms in the middle of the school year and become panicky. The parents are used to seeing the teacher in front of the room; they expect silence and little movement. Nothing in their backgrounds prepares them to know what to look for in a student-centered classroom, where the youngsters have many choices and considerable latitude in developing their own programs. Frequently they feel that they are walking into a chaotic situation that is out of the control of the teacher. They are also sure that no learning can be taking place in such a classroom.

The parents' usual response to this situation is to run to the principal and ask to have their child transferred to another class. If the teacher hasn't explained to the parent how learning can be observed in an open classroom, the child will be transferred, and doubts about the value of open learning will be planted in the minds of many of the other students and their parents as well. A few instances of this nature will provide the principal with sufficient cause to come down hard on the teacher and, if the teacher is not tenured, release him or her after the contract is up.

Explaining the nature of one's classroom to parents sometime during the middle of the school year will not avoid this problem. Parents ought to know what to expect from a teacher's classroom from the beginning of the year. They will then be able to go along with what is happening and know what to look for when they visit the room; or, if they do not like what will be happening, get a transfer for their child before the year begins. This takes away from the teacher the onus of being accused of having wasted the child's time, or done him harm, or let him fall behind, which are the usual excuses parents give for transferring their children.

A few years ago, I received a letter from Ken Bierly, a teacher at the Wildflecken American Elementary School in Wildflecken, West Germany (the school is for United States Army dependents), explaining how he educated his students' parents to accept an open learning situation.

Ken invited all of his students' parents to make a visit to his class an evening before school opened. A great effort was made to bring *all* the parents out. He then prepared his classroom to illustrate the kinds of activities his students would be participating in during the year. He also set up coffee and cookies and handed a mimeographed booklet to all of the parents as they arrived. The cover page reads:

> Dear Parents,
> Welcome to Room 2. We believe that this is a room where people can learn in an open and pleasant atmosphere. Tonight . . . I am

going to describe some basic parts of what's happening in Room 2. Please fill out the survey at the back of the booklet. Sit anywhere, and I hope you enjoy this evening and will learn about what we are doing here.

Help yourself to coffee and goodies whenever you like.

Ken Bierly

The tone of this first page tries to put the parents at ease. They are invited to sit where they like and are told that they are free to get coffee and cookies whenever they feel the need. The teacher is initiating the parents into his open classroom by offering them the same kinds of choices he offers their children.

The rest of the booklet contains:

1. An analysis of the background of open learning in the form of a series of questions and answers. Some sample questions are:

   a) What is the background that has led to the current activities in Room 2?
   b) What is the failure cycle and how can it be broken?
   c) What is the structure/freedom controversy?
   d) How does "process" learning differ from "content" learning?

The answers to these questions explain to the parents some of Piaget's ideas and give them a sense that what Ken is trying in his classroom has been tried elsewhere and has worked.

2. A statement of his objectives as a teacher, which revolve around his role as an adult whose concern is to help children learn and facilitate their growth.

3. A concrete description of the activities and learning materials available to his students.

4. An anecdotal description of a sample week, so that the parents can get an idea of what youngsters can do in an open situation.

5. Samples of his students' work from the previous year, as well as a description of the procedures he uses to evaluate student progress and participation, and report to the parents.

6. A section entitled *What You Can Do To Help Your Child* that reads as follows:

   a) Visit our classroom. Observe. Come any time.
   b) Ask what your child is doing.

c) Offer to help him or her with homework.

d) Question the teacher's philosophies and activities.

e) Keep the teacher informed of your views and objectives. Help establish and maintain three-way communication: home-school-child.

f) Offer to come to school to speak to the kids or have them visit you where you work.

g) Invite other children to your home to study or discuss school or just talk.

h) Encourage your child to read or become involved in *something*.

i) Help us make our school an important and participating part of our community.

7. A final section containing an annotated bibliography of books on open learning that the teacher has available for the parents to borrow, as well as a survey of parents' attitudes toward schools and ideas about learning.

This document assumes that parents are serious and intelligent individuals who care about their children and who can learn themselves. It anticipates many questions that the parents will have about Room 2, and gives the parents many hints about what to look for when they visit the school. It also invites them to participate in the learning processes that develop in the classroom.

Of course, what comes across from this document is that the teacher knows what he is about and therefore can write and speak with confidence and authority about his classroom. His document is not abstract or theoretical; it does not sound as if he read a chic book and adopted a new idea overnight.

The booklet is very specific about Room 2 and, because of that, it is convincing. Beginning teachers will find it harder to make a case to parents before the school year begins, but that is no reason not to try. It is better to go to the parents first and explain to them what you are attempting to do, than to have them storm into your classroom and demand to know what you think you are putting over on them and their children.

DEALING WITH FEELINGS—
ONE'S OWN AND THE STUDENTS'

There is no doubt in my mind that factors at work in my personality that I deny, push away, or am only vaguely aware of affect my work in the classroom. For example, I remember sitting at home some Sunday evenings, sipping wine and talking to my wife about books, music, politics—about anything but children and school. And I remember thinking before going to bed how nice it would be to stay home and make love all the next day, or to go to the park and walk around, or read an adult book for a change. The next morning I usually felt slightly angry and resentful on the way to school, and in my fantasies I fled from the school or destroyed it.

I also remember other Sundays, working like mad to prepare for Monday, putting together all kinds of materials for the students, impatient for the week to start, angry at the students when the week started because they weren't as enthusiastic about what I had prepared for them as I was.

During the last three years, while teaching a combined kindergarten and first grade, I've spent a lot of time thinking about the ways in which my and other adults' feelings and attitudes affect our work with children in the classroom. It is a great strain to deny our feelings and to be constant over five hours every day, five days a week. The easiest modes to fall into consist of praising students who obey us and blaming or tearing down those who don't. I remember screaming at students for being bad, when I really just wished they would leave me alone. I also remember praising students when they did just what I wanted, although I knew that they weren't learning anything other than how to please me and cash in later on my positive feelings toward them. I wasn't a mean or nasty or evil person. It was just that the pressure of being with students occasionally got to me, and when I began teaching I didn't know how to tell them that. I was feeling my way as a teacher. I looked to the other teachers for models; they were yelling, screaming, praising, or retreating to the toilet or teachers' lunchroom, and I fell into that pattern for a while. As soon as I got my bearings and developed some trust with the students, I could be much more natural, but that took me two years of learning how to teach, while being paid and recognized as a fully qualified teacher.

These situations took place nine and ten years ago. Now there are a number of nontraditional teaching situations where teachers do not have to feel unnatural and repressed. Most of the time. In open classrooms, free schools, and other alternative learning situations, emphasis is frequently put upon teachers being open and natural with their students. Teachers learn to spend time in so-called affective learning and are often less inhibited about telling their students how they feel as well as about encouraging the students to express feelings. Learning then becomes possible within the context of a generally permissive school or school system, particularly if learning is seen as understanding new and often frightening things and opening up difficult and unresolved questions. There are dangers in being open too, however, or in using openness with the students to involve them with our own personal adult problems. There is a thin line between being open in the service of our students and being open in the service of our own needs. Often we find out too late that some students are sucked into our lives without our really intending it.

I know teachers who, lusting for love, have offered love to students who took the offer more seriously and on a different level than intended. I know others who convinced young people that they, the teachers, would be around for years and years to give support, only to move away emotionally when their own lives became more settled or interesting.

Openness, naturalness, and closeness are all necessary with young people, especially if a person is serious about remaking this culture and society in a humane and just way. Rather than abandon these virtues because they are difficult and dangerous, I think it is important to be aware of some of the problems they present and to continually examine, define, and redefine in concrete terms the nature and quality of relationships with individuals and groups of students. I find it important to be hard on myself in order to avoid burdening my students with my own hang-ups.

There are no firm guidelines to help one function with sanity and responsibility. I can only describe some things I have seen, mention some mistakes I have made and observed, and make some tentative suggestions. There is a danger in needing to have all our students love, or pretend to love us. Love is a bonus in personal relationships. The most we can expect is respect, which cannot be forced but can only be developed through our acts. Love is a very loose term that often passes in so-called hip culture for agreement in style and in common opposition to some loosely defined notion of "straight" living. I know a number of hip, politically radical young white teachers whose first words to their ghetto-trapped students were, "I love you all." One student said to me, "That teacher said he loved me and he didn't even know me. The dude must be out of his mind."

In my teaching career I have come to love a small number of my students and have tried to minimize that love in the classroom by being fair to everyone. I have obligations to try to set up a sensible, open, and caring learning environment for all of my students, and not to pretend to love all of them or to act in special ways toward the ones I really do love. Of course, the special feelings teachers have for some students can never be fully suppressed. The students know who the teacher's pets are, even if the terminology and ideology pretend that there are no pets. Personal preferences are more likely to be accepted if we are just to everyone. In any case, fairness is not so difficult and ambitious as loving everyone.

I happen to like mischievous, wild, and independent people. Quiet is not my mode. I respect the calm and inner depth of silent people, but get educated by the loud, stylish troublemakers. These preferences sneak out in my relationships with students, and I have had to learn to give my time and concern to all of the young people I work with, not just to those who give me pleasure. All teachers have to face their own personal affinities and at the same time hold them in check so that they do not destroy, deny, or deceive students who do not strike some responsive note in their souls.

Another danger teachers face is wanting their students to understand them. Some teachers make themselves the curriculum, talking all the time about their marital problems, financial woes, or therapy sessions. They focus on themselves and forget about the students, while thinking it is open and groovy to be so honest with their students.

Young people love to hear stories about the lives of their elders.

My own children often ask me to tell a story about when I was young, about my friends, about my life before them, about meetings and work. And stories are wonderful to tell and wonderful to hear. But stories are different from confessions. Perhaps I am uptight and old-fashioned in believing that part of my life has to remain private and not at all understood by anyone except, perhaps, myself—but I do believe it. I believe further that young people ought not to be subjected to the problems of all of the adults they happen to be thrust in with in unnatural settings such as school. Young people need much more to understand themselves, each other, their parents, their community. The teacher might be understood, too, but school is not the world, the teacher is not the only model of adult life, and the main goal of schooling is to enable young people to get out of school able to do something they value and can give to others.

A subtle variant of wanting to be understood is wanting to be pitied. Some adults want young people to feel sorry for them, to recognize their weaknesses, and to be kind to them. Most teachers who take this stance with their students get wiped out quickly in schools where the students come from poor families. In middle-class schools, however, mutual self-pity is a fashionable mode of existence, and teachers who assume this mode can become popular with students who need desperately to feel stronger and wiser than some adults. But pity often leads to scorn, and teachers who adopt this mode are likely to find themselves rejected and mocked in private by their students. If you feel sorry for yourself, you really shouldn't be a teacher and put that sad defeat on anyone else.

A number of teachers want to politicize their students. I do too. I've tried over and over, and have found that the more dogmatic I get about my politics, the less the students pay attention to me. On the other hand, the more opportunity the students have to discover how political stances are developed and to experience political action, the more willing they are to take a position.

I have experienced a number of silly disappointments because I wanted my students to become radical. I wanted young people of fourteen, fifteen, sixteen, and seventeen to develop the political attitudes I developed after ten years of struggle, without going through anything themselves. I failed to realize or remember that their priorities and perspectives were not the same as mine. They needed to learn how to make love, how to live away from home, how to determine which adults to respect and believe, how to deal with money. I could not provide any shortcut to social commitment, and they did not want to take any risk that did not make sense to them. The students I am talking about were in an alternative secondary school in Berkeley. They were hip in the sense that they had long hair, smoked dope, wore fine leather boots, played rock. They had the money to indulge themselves in being hip, but didn't know anything about being radical in the sense of caring about the lives of people who did not have the luxury of being hip. I know no certain way to get white middle-class students to care about a world beyond themselves. But my anger and impatience and my radical stance did not help much, because in an important way it excluded the students and made light of their needs as they perceived them. A number of teachers who work with students from poor families fall into similar traps. They want their students to become militant, while all the students want to do is get some money and a job that will free them of poverty.

Some students do become politically aware in high school. For most others, political awareness and radical commitment emerge, if at all, from experiences at work and on the street, not from school. That does not mean that teachers should not help their students become aware of radical alternatives to the institutions and modes of life common in this society. Rather, it means that, though awareness can be facilitated by a teacher, commitment cannot be manufactured in the classroom. One thing that can be done is to adopt projects that take the students into the community to work on real problems. The Saint Paul Open School in St. Paul, Minnesota set up a student run consumer affairs center, and a group of students successfully fought a three-year battle to stop a large factory from polluting. This kind of activism does a great deal to expose students to the economic and political realities of our society.

Small things in a teacher's life tend to disturb classrooms—things like hangovers, fits of depression or elation, spring fever, occasional boredom, weariness of being with young people so much, and so forth. Slight discomfort can easily be turned into an excuse to stay away from school, to develop imaginary maladies, or to create rationalizations about the need for teachers, as well as students, to have choices—and therefore, the right of the teacher to choose to be absent a good deal.

I have found that often it is better to force myself to go in and tell the students how I feel than to stay away. On some days, of course, it is impossible to be around anyone, and therefore I have to be absent. But it is possible to function with a little bit of pain, and it is important for teachers not to pamper themselves or become chronic complainers. If teaching becomes a draining burden, we should prepare ourselves for other work.

Another hang-up some teachers have is the need to be a martyr. Some people hate teaching, hate schools, act as if they are fed up with the students all the time, and yet feel that the reason they continue to teach is to save the students. Often the students do not feel they are being saved and do not like being reminded constantly of how much the teacher is sacrificing to save them.

I have taught for eleven years, though never more than three years in a row or three years at one place. I can take young people and schools in three-year doses. After that time I get restless and need to do something else. A useful guideline I have followed is that whenever, over a period of a month, I feel no joy at seeing my students, drag myself to school every day, and long to stay home or run away, it is time for me to leave the next year.

Often large crises in our lives affect our work with young people. Love affairs break up, friends die, a new political obscenity develops, some insane violence comes to haunt one's life. These occasions have to change the rhythm of life—death or the end of an affair have to be mourned; political anguish is real and necessary if we are to remain human. I have found that in moments of crisis I can acknowledge my feelings to my students and that they can respect my experiences. The fact that adults experience pain and that some can cope with it has often led young people to talk about their pain, about what they see adults experiencing, and about ˙ what they themselves experience. The important thing is not to turn personal pain into an excuse for rejecting or abandoning students, or an excuse for expecting your students to solve problems that you as an adult should solve.

It is extremely difficult to develop that combination of consistency, strength, and openness that seems to enable teachers to work effectively with young people. There are many hang-ups that all of us have as adults and many temptations to bring all of them into the classroom. This is especially true of adults who work in open settings, where the expression and display of feeling is part of the fabric of life. We have to become tough with ourselves and realize that teaching in an open setting does not give us license to play out our fantasies or fulfill all of our needs through the lives of young people. Our job as teachers should be to turn our students on to themselves, to each other, and to all things there are to learn about in the world.

LOSING CONTROL

There are days when I simply cannot keep the class together. Maybe it's the rain or something that happened on the bus. I can never tell, but I have to deal with the immediate fact that most of the children don't care to be in school that day, much less do any work. Things aren't so bad during the times that we have individual or small-group activity. But once a morning I bring the whole class together and either present a new activity or new material that is available in the room, or continue a discussion we have had, or deal with some group problems. On the days that I am talking about there are always a number of students who roll around on the floor or hit someone or make jokes or try to provoke me into screaming and yelling and sending them out of the room. I find that losing my temper never helps anything, and sending students out of the room often leads them to cause trouble for other teachers and students. Consequently, I have developed a number of ways of flowing with the class's restlessness and turning it into something productive.

I first discovered something that settled the class down one day when things were so out of control that I was ready, despite my best intentions and strongest will, to grab and shake a particularly troublesome student. I moved toward him with the most menacing look I could muster and picked him up brusquely. The class turned silent, waiting for the hammer to fall. I gritted my teeth and then turned the student over my lap and raised my hand as if to spank him. Then I lowered my hand as slowly as possible and proceeded to mime spanking the child, whispering to him that his role was to pretend to cry. He let out the most drawn-out and mournful moans. The other students, catching on immediately, said that they wanted their turns at being spanked. I obliged a few of the students and then asked everyone to sit down and told them we would try something new. There would have been no use going back to what I had originally intended for that day. The class sat quietly and expectantly, which surprised me. I asked two of the most restless students to stand up and get ready to fight each other. Then I told them that they could only move in slow motion and not touch each other. They had to mime a battle. They also had to control their bodies so that they never broke out of the slow rhythm of the mime. I asked one of the students to practice, and she quickly realized that it wasn't such an easy thing to slow up her body and take conscious control over her movement. After the practice the students fought the mock-battle. Then I asked them to pretend to embrace. Next I asked the whole class to stand up as slowly as they could and raise their hands as high as they could, and when they couldn't go any higher to get up on their tiptoes and pretend that they could take off and fly.

After the exercise was over, the students fell on the rug and giggled and rolled around. This time it wasn't a few naughty ones, it was the class, which after a while quieted down and asked for more improvisations. I suggested that they all lie down on their backs and close their eyes. Then I asked them to imagine they were asleep and told them I would become a dream master for the moment and suggest they live in a dream for a while. I suddenly filled their dream world with water and said we were all underwater and could only move the way fish moved. I suggested they begin to test themselves in the water and swim around and begin to think of the kind of fish they were—whether they were sharks or minnows, beautiful tropical fish or fearsome blowfish with poison spines. The spell was broken by a damned fire drill, but I remained amazed at the self-discipline some of the most defiant and undisciplined children in the class had shown.

A few days later (it was the dreary rainy season in northern California) things got out of hand again. I decided to go along with the physical restlessness of the students, and instead of punishing them for being restless asked everyone to stand on the rug and shout as loud as they could for thirty seconds. Then I asked them to be quiet for the same length of time. Then we ran in place and pretended to be fighting for the same amount of time, and then pretended to be walking slowly down the street, shaking hands with our friends. This time more elaborate improvisations followed this warm-up. Students mimed driving their parents' cars, picking up buildings, taking each other's pictures, flying airplanes—taking all the power of grown-ups.

Slowly I began to integrate the development of physical self-control into our morning rug time. Usually we spent five minutes a day at mime, that is, at slowing down or speeding up movements and developing ideas and themes through the body without the mediating function of words.

Things rested there until one day I noticed one of the students walking up to the bookcase in slow motion and picking out a book and sitting down to read it, all in mime. I asked what was happening, and he said that reading scared him, which was true. He threw books on the floor and would do anything to avoid having to face a book or workbook or anything that smacked of reading. He said that maybe it was because he was too fast and too angry. He decided to use mime and see what would happen if he read slowly. He also said that I had to get away because I made him nervous. Then he slowly went back to the book.

Often school is too fast or too slow for students. They are not allowed to pace themselves and are never given the idea that it is possible to come to understand and to develop their own pace and style of learning. The fast learners are rewarded, the slow ones punished. And yet what difference does it make if one learns to read quickly or slowly? If you learn to read, the quality of your ability is not dependent upon the speed with which you acquired the skill. I have three children. One talked at eleven months, another at eighteen months. Now that they are all over five, you can't tell the difference. The speed with which they learned to read doesn't make any difference in their lives or their ability to communicate. We as teachers have to understand and support our students as they develop their own styles of learning. And we have to give them ways of slowing themselves down if that is what they need, or going faster if that is what they feel they have to do.

Control over the body is not divorced from control over the mind. As students practice controlling their bodies and learn how to experiment with different paces, they also learn indirectly how to control their minds. Teachers have to learn how to make the bridge, to use the body to teach the mind, and the mind to integrate with the body.

BEING OUT OF CONTROL

Sometimes it is not the students who are out of control, restless, or confused about what is expected of them. Teachers face the same behavior problems as their students and have to be open enough to admit it.

One of the first-graders in my class two years ago called me Herbie the Grouch every time I got angry at him. David sometimes came in sullen and angry. He would push other children out of his way, hit them in the back, or knock over their games and scribble on their work. On other days he would be the gentlest, most charming and considerate person. It was impossible to tell from one day to the next how he would be in the morning.

I took to watching him walk into the room in the morning. In our class the students come in a few at a time and for the first hour can choose from many different activities. During that hour the adults (usually myself and a co-teacher or student teacher) call the students one at a time to do individualized reading, and we have a chance to spend a few minutes a day with every child. David was usually the first student I called to read, or at least the one I looked at first. I watched the way he walked into the room, noted the set of his brow, how he held his hands and fists, how his eyes scanned the room. At the first sign of aggression I pounced:

"David, today you'll take care of yourself . . ."
"David, you read first today . . ."
"David, keep your hands to yourself . . ."
"David, do something . . . sit down . . . enjoy yourself . . ."
"David, don't . . ."

Grouch, Grouch, Grouch—that's what he called me, and the other students picked up on it too. I didn't like being called Grouch and tried to joke off the name. However, I couldn't let him continue to harass other students and destroy their work. I had to accept a minimally grouchy role in order to allow the other students the peace and calm necessary for them to make choices and function in our open environment.

It became easy after a while to set limits on David's behavior by sitting on top of him at the beginning of the day. But there were problems with my behavior. Sometimes during the days before Christmas I came to school tired and impatient and found myself grouching at David and some of the other students in the hope that it would make my day easier. The difference between grouching to set and maintain sensible limits in the class, that is, to insure that bullying and the destruction of work didn't develop, and grouching to make my day easier wasn't always clear. I could sense something was wrong on those latter days because some of the students would imitate me, and they, too, would go around grouching and complaining at the slightest thing. Those days we seemed like a tired, touchy group of people.

Teachers sometimes are tired, obsessed, troubled by things that have nothing to do with events in the classroom. It is impossible to conceal these feelings from the students, especially in an informal learning environment where the adults and the young people have time to talk to each other. Ways have to be found to bring these feelings out in the open rather than try to force silence and obedience on the class so the teacher can relax.

David and other students would look at me occasionally and tell me to turn the grouch off and point out that they hadn't done anything wrong. They showed me that on some days I let them play around or make noise and that on other days I didn't. It was the grouch factor, which David suggested was located somewhere in the back of my brain, that was responsible for my behavior. I immediately picked up on his suggestion and said that there *was* a grouch factor. I went to the blackboard and drew a head and a brain. At the back of the brain I labeled a section "the grouch's house," and the class sat down and we began to discuss what brought out the grouch in me (and in the others as well, for the idea of a grouch in the brain allowed many of the students to acknowledge that they, too, had days with their grouches out).

We decided that there were inside reasons and outside reasons that set the grouch off. I admitted that sometimes I grouched because I came to school in a bad mood. Other times it was because some of the students were messing up with each other and I had to set limits. David even acknowledged that he woke up some mornings with his grouch out, and those mornings it was as if his grouch activated mine. The discussion was quite sophisticated, more, certainly, than I had suspected five- and six-year-olds capable of. We were able to use the grouch idea as an image to enable us to think about and analyze behavior.

The notion of a grouch factor even changed behavior in the class. One day we speculated on what keeps the grouch happy, and the students suggested jokes, snacks, praise, isolation. We talked about ways we had of bringing angry feelings under control. I suggested that the students remind me when my grouch was showing and told them I would do the same for them. It was no longer necessary for me to look at David for signs of aggression or to put a moral interpretation on his behavior (despite myself, he was emerging in my mind as a "bad" student, even though he was one of the most intelligent and competent students in the class). It was his grouch, and I could appeal to it when he came in angry. Moreover, since it was his grouch, he began to assume responsibility for its behavior and learned ways to leave other students alone or scribble on his own work or go outside and break a stick instead of a game or a sculpture. The students could also remind me of my feelings, and I could deal with them without feeling insulted or injured by the students' criticism.

Indirect ways of discussing feelings help de-charge a situation. I have found that young children use superheroes, animals, imaginary friends, and astrological symbols as tokens of thought that enable them to deal in complex ways with pain and conflict, and also to assume responsibility for their own behavior. Whenever some collective problem arises in our class, I have found that the best way to deal with it is to start with a story or fable or adventure that embodies the problem. Then we can deal with the problem in the class through the story, causing no one to lose face and everyone to be able to talk about responsibility.

I have found the following books rich sources of tales and legends that I have drawn on in my work with five- and six-year-olds:

> *The Adventures of Spider* by Joyce Cooper Arkhurst (Boston: Little, Brown, 1964)
> *More Adventures of Spider* by Joyce Cooper Arkhurst (New York: Scholastic Book Serv., 1972)
> *The Dermis Probe,* Idries Shah (New York: Dutton, 1971)
> *Folktales of Mexico,* edited and translated by Americo Paredes (Chicago: Univ. of Chicago Press, 1970)
> *A Treasury of American Folklore,* edited by B. A. Botkin (New York: Crown, 1944)
> *A Harvest of World Folk Tales,* edited by Milton Rugoff (New York: Viking, 1949)
> *The Wise Men of Chelm,* Samuel Tenenbaum (New York: Yoseloff, 1965).

FATIGUE

There are days of grouchiness in the classroom, and there are also weeks of fatigue. No teacher should feel guilty for being tired if he or she has planned, prepared, and functioned in a way that nurtures the students. For all of us there are times of the year when teachers and students get tired of each other and the routines and rituals they have fallen into. This fatigue is indicated in many different ways.

Teachers take their excused absences more frequently during these times. Students and teachers know exactly how many days there are to the next holiday. And everybody remembers what happened on Monday and Friday, but forgets the content of Tuesday, Wednesday, and Thursday. Weekends seem shorter and weeks longer. Even the most interesting subjects seem flavorless, and the most open classrooms oppressive.

I generally experience my doldrums in late November, early February, and mid-May. It is almost as if the cycles in my classroom life come to an end at three-month intervals, and then the students and I need time off from each other to think about what has happened between us and reflect upon what was learned or felt in the classroom.

I also experience times of quietude and aimlessness with my students after we have done something particularly exciting or important. For example, when we master a play or think through a math problem that has stumped us for weeks, or manage to resolve a particularly delicate group conflict or create a piece of work that moves us all, we are reluctant to talk about the experience or to come together immediately to begin new work.

I know when something moves me particularly, I want time to savor it, think about it, hold it in my mind and imagination. My students have told me that they feel the same way.

In most classrooms, however, there is no time to reflect or hold at a particular point and drift for a while. There is little time to celebrate communal achievement or discuss and respect boredom and weariness. Yet it seems to me that it is crucial that the rhythm of the school year be adjusted to the organic rhythms of individual classes. Learning cannot be parceled out evenly over all the days of the year, and every day cannot be expected to contain the same amount of material to be covered. There must be peaks and valleys, variations in the quality and quantity of work done at different times.

It is hardly possible to go along studying history or doing math at the same steady pace throughout a school year without destroying the excitement the subjects can have for students or making rote memorization take the place of understanding. A particularly keen historical insight or an elegant line of mathematical reasoning ought to be savored. Sometimes it takes time to understand a particular concept, and that means pausing for a while and thinking it through.

There are times when students will do dull, regular work in order to master a subject or a skill. I have seen students practicing on musical instruments, or drawing or writing for two hours at a time, just trying to get things right. However, even the most dedicated musician or writer grows weary of work or practice at times and needs a rest, a change of pace. The same is true for young people.

As things are presently structured in the public schools, however, it is impossible to set aside time to relax and change the daily routine of life. Trips have to be justified; even walks around the block have to be described in terms of educational objectives. People cannot do things simply because they may seem to be nice or interesting things to do, or because there is a need for a change of pace. Yet we have to relax, to celebrate something, to do things because they seem pleasant or interesting. It is as valuable for students and teachers to spend a nice day together walking and talking as it is for them to go to a special exhibit and see how people in another world live.

Often there is as much need for a change of scene in the classroom as for a change of pace. The decor of the room may become boring after a while, or it might reflect activities no longer relevant to the students' interests. I know that I feel the same way about the decor of my study. Every once in a while, usually after I feel that a period in my life or writing has passed, I feel an urge to change the environment and start anew.

The same thing happens in the classroom. There are times when the students begin to complain about the room. It seems dull, the posters and work they have put up are no longer interesting, the desks or chairs or cushions or couches seem uncomfortable.

At these times of spatial boredom I have found that the only thing that works is a ritual housecleaning. The students and I take apart the classroom, throw out all the old posters and decorations, move all the chairs and tables out of the room, and then we begin again. A day of housecleaning, followed by a day of rebuilding the classroom environment, almost always serves to renew our interest in the room and in our lives together.

There is a need for constant renewal of interest and energy in the classroom. And there is a need for time to rest and do nothing. When young people work hard at learning (and it often happens if they are free to learn what they care to know), there are times when they are exhausted. There are other times when they are too filled with what they have just learned to be ready to move immediately on to something else, something new.

It is crucial that teachers respect the personal, and often private, nature of learning and enable their students to take the time to think and reflect upon what they are doing. Time cannot be objectified and students required to learn on schedule. Nor can space be set once and for all without regard for the comfort of people who live within it. The classroom must be responsive to the pace at which students learn and to their need for a rich and changing environment.

PRIVATE SPACES

When I was in the sixth grade, the teacher used to propose special math problems and give us a half hour to solve them. Any student who got the right answers in that time was given a special high grade. I never got any of the problems right and kicked myself for being so stupid.

I used to take the special math problems home with me, hide in my room and think about them. At home, alone, able to listen to music and walk around, I could solve the problems. In school, with all the other students around me, with the silence in the room and the pressure of grades and time, I couldn't think about math. All I thought about was not getting the right answer and being thought stupid by the teacher and the other kids.

When I taught the sixth grade, there were many fights in the class. Students often defied me, but more often they fought with each other. I had to resolve the fights as quickly as possible. There was no place to go to work out the problems behind the fights or let the combatants rest and talk to each other.

I remember a particularly bad fight between two boys who had liked each other very much up until the moment the battle broke out in the classroom. I wanted to go and talk with the boys, but that was impossible. There was no one to watch my class, and even if there had been, the only place we could talk was in the hall, which was full of movement and very unprivate.

During the time I taught in New York City, the union won preparation periods for elementary school teachers. We had an hour a day to prepare lessons and do research on curriculum. The problem was that the only place we had to do it was in the teachers' lunchroom, which was filled with people drinking coffee and gossiping or just resting and looking for a conversation.

Just this year I have talked with a number of students about how to make the school environment more comfortable and welcoming. Almost without exception the students want spaces that are private, in which they can be alone, or alone with a few friends, and talk and work and think. One of their main complaints about school is that there is no provision for the privacy and personal lives of students. It is even so bad in some schools that the doors are removed from the stalls in the student toilets, though not in the faculty johns.

There are certain things best done in private, among them, perhaps, thinking, creating, solving problems and conflicts, and resting. Schools don't have private places for the students or teachers to think or work alone or develop environments that fit their personal styles of learning and teaching. They don't have places where people can come together in small groups and work free from public scrutiny.

The classroom is a particularly public place. The space is open, with no private corners or separate divisions for people to be alone in. Yet it is the classroom where we expect and often demand that students think and solve problems and create poems and stories and deal with their conflicts with other students.

Let us look at these different activities separately. How do people usually go about thinking and solving problems, creating works of art, and solving conflicts outside the classroom?

Thinking is a complex activity that no one has been able to quantify, to describe fully. It is clear, however, that different people find themselves able to think best in different circumstances. Some people can think best with music on; others need complete silence. Some people do their best thinking while walking, others while sitting in an easy chair, or lying down, or sitting in a restaurant or public square watching passers-by.

Problems are solved in many different ways. Some people

dream up answers; others need a pen in their hand or another person to push them into thinking of a solution.

Making a work of art is an even more eccentric activity. Artists and writers have special conditions and environments under which they work. Some can work with other people present; others need to be completely alone. I cannot write with anyone else around. I also have to write on a certain size paper and with a special pen. This is not just my madness. We all seek the most comfortable environments in which to work. Robert Creeley, the poet, has expressed what I am getting at in a speech he gave at a poetry conference in Vancouver about the contexts in which poets create their work. He said:

> What I'm trying to say is don't start thinking of writing as some particular activity leading to some particular effect for some particular purpose. It is just as relevant what size paper you use, as whether or not you think you are writing a sonnet. In fact, it's more relevant. And this aspect of your activity ought to be, you ought to be aware of it. . . . In other words, if you want to write with a paper like this, please DO! If you find yourself stuck with habits of articulation, try doing something else, try shifting the physical context.*

Solving conflicts is as personal as creating a work of art. I do not feel easy dealing with someone's problem in public, and as a teacher I was always embarrassed by the need to deal with the problems of two or three students with all the other students present.

It is important to build private spaces into existing classrooms. Right now I am experimenting with the possibility of creating private corners and little rooms within existing rooms. Fabric is magical. A few muslin dividers hanging from the ceiling can create private spaces. Clothing closets can be turned into private rooms. Even rugs on the floors can mark private spaces. The hall outside a classroom can be partitioned off and turned into a series of private spaces as well. Portable Japanese walls or ingenious room dividers can be used. The classroom can be changed into a complex

---

* Robert Creeley, "Contexts of Poetry," *Audit* 5, no. 1 (Spring 1968), p. 7

environment accommodating private as well as public experience. There is no simple formula to achieve this transformation. It is up to the ingenuity of individual teachers. We have to take the environments that we are given as teachers and change them so that they will be fine places for living and learning.

Two books worth consulting on developing learning environments are *Farallones Scrapbook,* edited by Sim van der Ryn (New York: Random House, 1972) and *Found Spaces and Equipment for Children's Centers* (this is available from the Ford Foundation Educational Facilities Laboratory, 850 Third Avenue, New York, N.Y. 10022).

4. THE POLITICS OF TEACHING

KNOWING THE HIERARCHY

SOLARO IS A suburb of San Francisco. It is not a middle-class community, however. Most of the families live in mobile home parks or in old farm buildings badly in need of repair. There is one middle-income development that is being completed. The Luther Burbank elementary school serves all of Solaro. The school was very traditional until a new principal arrived a few years ago. She believed that the atmosphere of the school might have something to do with the fact that most of the children neither read nor wrote with any degree of competence by the end of the sixth grade. She decided to develop a warm, informal atmosphere at the school, to initiate programs that interested the students and allowed them a great deal of choice and responsibility for their own learning. She initially had a very resistant staff and suspicious community. They didn't want any "hippie ideas" tried on their children. The words "open" or "free" raised the specter of permissiveness, which they identified with chaos. On the other hand, anything that worked in ways they could understand—that is, taught their children to read and write and not be failures in school—was okay with them. So, without using any rhetoric, the principal began to make the school a better place for the children. A number of old teachers retired, and the principal replaced them with experienced teachers who had progressive ideas. The first young teacher she hired came well recommended from a teacher training institution that specialized in preparing its students to teach in open classrooms.

John arrived with a station wagon full of math and science apparatus (cuisinaire rods, balance beams, microscopes, all kinds of discovery learning kits, and so on). He was extremely energetic and enthusiastic, and also extremely political. He took it as his mission to convince working-class children and parents that they were oppressed and needed to organize to change the society. He had also never had his own classroom before nor had he worked at a school in transition.

He made two mistakes on the first day of school. He put out most of his equipment and told the children they could do whatever they wanted with it. Then at lunchtime he put down two of the traditional teachers for not having heard of Jerome Bruner or Jean Piaget.

The students did what they wanted with the equipment—broke it and threw it all around the room. They began gently, dropping a few cuisinaire rods, breaking a microscope slide. They waited for John to stop them, to set some limits. He didn't, and by lunchtime the room was a mess. John rationalized this as indicating that working-class children needed to break things because they didn't experience freedom at home. He would teach them how to be free.

This first mistake was the less serious of the two because there was time for him to learn about the students and come to understand their needs if only he could survive at the school. But after the first day, the clique of traditional teachers decided that John would be their first test case in trying to oppose the principal. They saw him as very vulnerable, though he was at that point supremely confident in his pedagogical and political radicalism. They were right, despite the fundamental rightness and humanity of his ideas.

John made many little mistakes that he never thought about. He was not attuned to the social system that existed among the teachers, nor the ties that teachers who had been around for a while had within the community. His politics were abstract rather than concrete, and eventually he put the principal, who brought him to the school and wanted to support him, in a position of having to let him go to preserve the work she was doing. For example, he mentioned to his pupils that he disapproved of their former teachers and of traditional teaching in general, not realizing that the students would tell their parents, some of whom would call up the teachers he criticized. At the first parents' meeting he introduced himself to the parents and gave them a lecture on open education, which was received politely but coldly. The parents knew the principal had hired him, and even though they felt suspicious, they were willing to judge him on what he did rather than what he said.

He made other mistakes nobody told him about, like putting down Little League baseball, mocking teenagers who were obsessed by cars, or girls who spent all their time prettying themselves. He didn't get to know or establish trust within the school or community first, so for that whole year he remained an outsider. Nobody told him about the gossip or pointed out his enemies, or even warned him that a few parents, at the instigation of some teachers, were circulating a petition to have him fired. Just as he felt his teaching was coming together, that the students were coming to trust him and feel good about themselves as learners, the petition was presented to the principal. He spent the rest of the year fighting to survive. Eventually, a compromise was reached—he would finish the year and would not be given a bad recommendation to prejudice future employment, but he could not return.

John and I talked a lot about what happened to him, and more specifically about how thoroughly unprepared he was to deal with the community and the other teachers. His entire training had focused on how to function with students within the classroom, and yet survival turned out during his first year to depend upon how he dealt with other teachers and the community.

John's experience is far from unique. Many committed, energetic young teachers find themselves unable to survive the first few years within the social system of the school or within communities they do not know or understand. There may be good reasons not to survive—the staff of a school may be hopelessly oppressive to the students, and silence in the face of their actions would be intolerable without becoming an oppressor oneself. Or one might believe, as some critics of public schools do, that any contact, other than opposition, with public education is contaminating and in compliance with maintenance of the society as it is presently constituted. It is also possible that one simply cannot reach a certain kind of student or that a particular community is so alien and makes one so uncomfortable that it is the wrong place for one to be. However, if one does believe, as I do, that infiltrating and attempting to change public schools is one way to be involved in creating conditions for fundamental and humane change in this culture, then a prospective teacher has to know something about the rules, customs, and manners that govern the social system he or she will try to change. The teacher must also know how to learn about a community and become trusted and valued by the community.

This knowledge, combined with excellence in the classroom, might make it possible to establish a base within the school and community so that the teacher can begin to remake the school or, if necessary, develop the organization and power to take it over.

Here are some hints that might be useful to a beginning teacher who wants to make sense of the social world he or she might encounter at work. The school is a hierarchical social system, and many of the customs that one has to accept exist in order to maintain the hierarchy, at the top of which is the principal and at the bottom, almost without class or "untouchable" in some schools, are the pupils. The structure usually looks something like this:

principal

assistant principals–administrative assistants

specialists or curriculum coordinators

classroom teachers

regular substitute teachers

teachers' aides–playground supervisors

office help–the school secretary

custodial staff

students

The first thing to remember is that actual power at the school and knowledge of what is going on are not directly related to position in the hierarchy. Hierarchical position is more related to credentials and salary. In every school I have worked at or observed, the most knowledgeable and powerful person in terms of day-to-day functioning has been the school secretary. She has all the keys, knows what resources are available to the teachers, screens phone calls, sits in on administrative meetings, talks to most of the students, intercepts angry parents and gossips with contented ones. She is the schools' number one gatekeeper. Turn her off, put her down, ignore her, or show disrespect, and your life as a teacher can become miserable. Become her friend, and you will learn about things affecting you, and have someone who can introduce you to the factions that exist within the school, warn you when you are inadvertently out of bounds, and give you access to supplies that are hoarded or available to the principal's favorite teachers.

The school secretary is usually a bridge person as well as a gatekeeper. She passes messages informally from teacher to teacher, or teacher to administrator. For example, she lets her friends know when it is a good time to talk to the principal and when the principal is in a funk. It is important for young teachers to go out of their way not to antagonize her, even though at a later point she might turn out to be a very dangerous conservative force at the school that has to be opposed. My experience during political confrontations at school is that school secretaries divide the way most other people do—some radical, some conservative, and most trying to protect themselves and maintain the power they have.

Janitors or custodians often are second in control in terms of actual day-to-day power. They can make your life miserable by insinuating that your room is too dirty and you are making their work too hard. They can refuse to clean, reveal all sorts of things to the principal, make the book and supply closets inaccessible. One teacher in Oakland told me that he was prevented from rearranging the tables, desks, and bookcases in his room in order to open up things for his students because the janitors complained to the principal that it meant more work for them, and they threatened to refuse to clean the school at all.

On the other hand, the custodians and janitors have the keys and know where everything is; they can help you clean a messy room, and can support you by letting the principal know what a nice place your classroom is. A few years ago, I was running a weekend school for high school kids in New York while I was on the unofficial staff of the Horace Mann-Lincoln Institute at Teachers College, Columbia University. There were initially no facilities available for the students and myself until I became friendly with a few janitors and secretaries. After a while, they opened up a few rooms at Teachers College to us on Saturdays and Sundays, and provided us with paper and mimeograph supplies. On Friday nights they helped us use mimeograph machines and rip off enough paper to print a community magazine.

It may sound unlikely, but secretaries and janitors can become crucial figures in your effort to change the school. As opponents they can convince people that the clerical work is impossible, that the wear on the plant expensive. On the other hand, they can volunteer to help you and cover you during times of stress.

One more specific example: I know some people who tried to change the playground of an elementary school. They wanted to rip up the asphalt and plant a garden. They planned a climbing apparatus and a large sandbox. They had an architect draw up impressive plans and raised most of the money necessary to buy the materials. However, the janitors told the principal that the plan was not feasible and were so adamant in their opposition that the whole thing never got started.

A few years later, some of the people acted in a smarter way. They went to the janitorial staff first and asked their advice on how to make the playground more interesting for the students. The janitors joined the parents and some teachers in planning the playground and even donated their own labor. The finished playground looked a lot like the original plan, but some of the staff's additions were interesting. The janitors also took good care of their own handiwork.

One final comment about janitors and secretaries: the school should resemble a democratic community, and everyone whose life and work is affected ought to be involved in the decision-making process. This is not so farfetched. In England and more recently in the United States, there are a number of mental hospitals that have experimented with flattening out the hierarchy of doctor–nurse–orderly–janitor–patients, and developing collective decision making. The morale of the place improves, and everyone seems to benefit from a diversity of perspectives and attitudes. The same thing can become true in the school community (which includes the students, who, I guess, are analogous to the patients).

However, I have seen resistance to democratizing the governance of the school. In one case in Berkeley, a staff of elementary school teachers was outraged by the possibility of teachers' aides sitting in on faculty meetings. The question of the aides making decisions and having parity with the teachers was never raised. The very idea of their presence threatened the teachers' sense of self-esteem. Shaky professionals are hardly ready for anything resembling democracy. However, the school will never become an open community unless everyone, no matter what his or her role, has the opportunity to participate in decision making and has a forum to express ideas, beliefs, and feelings to all the other members of the community. Scorn or condescension toward secretaries and janitors is the kind of class prejudice that often drives a wedge between university-educated people and the people they believe they are trying to help.

One cut below the janitors in the school hierarchy are the students—the clients, as some systems-oriented educational professionals call them. (Others call the students, along with their parents, the "target population" of the school.) Students do not have the power to say no to any other people at the school in most instances. If an adult tells a student to do something, he must obey or he has violated the adult's role and is therefore, whatever his academic achievement might be, a bad student. The young people at the school are divided into good and bad students.

A good student is supposed to act in certain specified ways whenever in the presence of a teacher, administrator, or other adult. The code of student *behavior* takes precedence over academic performance and intelligence. It is crucial to understand that the good student is not to be confused with the bright student. Goodness is much more closely related to obedience than to academic accomplishment. Here is a summary of the code:

1. *A student must pretend to respect all the adults who work in professional roles at the school.* Insulting a janitor, for example, is usually considered a less serious offense than insulting a teacher.

Legislated respect demands certain ritual action. For example, since all adults must be respected, whether they deserve respect or not, a good student swallows pride and bears with the worst of adults. A good student addresses all teachers as Mr., Mrs., or Miss and never uses first names. A good student never jokes with the teacher or makes fun of the teacher or tells the teacher that he or she is wrong. All of those actions would show lack of respect.

2. *A good student must be willing to perform the craziest tasks,* such as asking permission to go to the toilet or to throw a piece of paper in the wastebasket. A good student must be willing to line up and sit down on command, to answer stupid questions in dull workbooks, to repeat facts that have no interest or significance, to fill out forms, take tests, run errands.

3. *A good student must accept his or her own inferiority and fear revealing his or her own innate stupidity.* The good student acts as if the teacher has superior knowledge and wisdom, while knowing that what the teacher actually has is a grade book and a conduct book. Fear must govern the good student's actions—fear of not being approved by the teacher, fear of not being able to perform, fear of being called dumb by the rest of the class at the instigation of the teacher, fear of being publicly shamed by giving a wrong answer.

4. *A good student will understand that his or her parents are collaborating with the teacher,* so that there is no alternative to obedience. The good student will feel trapped into conforming to the demands of adults and will after a while accept conformity as part of the nature of existence. However, usually there will be some residual resentment and so the good student, though having to be obedient, is allowed not to look happy all the time. Generally, even the good student will be allowed a few angry or bored facial expressions a day in class, though I know some very nervous teachers who insist that their students look happy and harass them into pretending to smile.

5. *Good students know that they must take no initiatives.* They must have a sense that all objections they make to anything that happens in school can only be made at the moment and in the form

permitted by the teacher or principal. I remember when I was president of the student body at the Bronx High School of Science in 1954. We had a particularly stormy meeting of the student council, which naturally was supervised by a faculty advisor. The students wanted to talk about the power of the principal, who was extremely autocratic and paternalistic, to veto all of our actions. The faculty advisor rose to inform us that the question was not one we could legitimately raise without the express permission of the principal, an obvious absurdity even for us students, who were good enough to be sanctioned as candidates for student government (a repository of good students). I was outraged at the moment and banged the gavel and ruled the faculty advisor out of order. There was a stunned silence in the room—I had violated Rules 1 through 5, and nobody knew what to do. Finally, the faculty advisor dissolved the meeting and went to his office with a few loyal and good students, and, I heard, cried. He said that such a thing never had happened before. Obviously, the explanation was that I was not really a good student, or, as he put it later on, I "let him down."

There are other initiatives not expected of students. For example, students are not expected to make social or sexual advances to teachers. They are not expected to initiate new areas of study or develop new lines to pursue in old areas of study. They are not expected or allowed to fix broken windows, paint peeling walls or ceilings, repaint or decorate the facades of school buildings. They are supposed to live sordidly until the adults get around to improving the school environment or else they will be stigmatized as bad students.

Being a good student can be crippling. It requires the suppression of good sense, the abandonment of initiative, the loss of intuition, the impoverishment of humor, the death of sensibility. Of course, what one loses or suppresses in the classroom can still be preserved at home or on the streets or in the playground if a student can bear the tension of a schizoid life. I have noticed a number of "good students" who, upon arriving home from school, immediately brutalize their younger brothers and sisters as if getting even for the oppression they are rewarded for undergoing at school.

Teachers are expected to enforce the code of student behavior.

This can be especially difficult if they encourage their students to develop good sense, use initiative, attend to their instincts, and express their feelings. There are times when one might have to choose between defending the code and showing solidarity with the other adults at the school, or defending a student and risking one's job. I have been in that situation a number of times. Often my students took the initiative and forced me to take a stand, to show them whether I meant my ideas about openness and justice or was just another hypocritical adult. One of the third grade teachers at a school I taught at in Harlem was a particularly brutal racist. He hated black children, perhaps hated all children, but since all the students were black, the hatred came out in overtly racist forms. He beat children, shoved them against the walls, called them "niggers." His idea was that you had to show "them" how tough you were in order to maintain discipline.

For some time I avoided thinking about him. However, my students kept bringing up the issue, and finally put it to me directly: do something about him, or you're the same as he is, as brutal and racist and willing to let us be hurt. I made the confrontation, and the other adults at the school made my life miserable. They agreed that the way he treated the students was wrong, but were even more offended by my breaking the code.*

Those students who are not good are, of course bad. Being bad at school is a painful position for students to be in, quite analogous to the position of the bad teacher which I found myself in. Most bad students accept the idea that there is something wrong with them and wish to be good, or are ready to give up on school altogether. This is just another way this culture pressures young people to fit in and keep quiet.

To stay sane many young people must act crazy and be defiant. However, there are sensible and non-self-destructive ways of being "bad." A few years ago I made a list of several principles for being a bad student with the intent of changing the school, rather than indulging or hurting oneself. I think most of them apply equally to

* If you are interested in ways in which events like these can push one to become committed to fundamental change, you might take a look at my *Half the House* (E. P. Dutton, 1974).

young teachers who are willing to challenge the system that pays them:

Four Principles of Being a Bad Student/Teacher

1. *Respect being a mutual thing, do not feel guilty about respecting only those adults that respect you.* Do not, however, be disrespectful just for the sake of it, or because a defiant attitude makes adults mad. Don't test your strength over adults in stupid and nonpolitical ways. From my perspective, respect means treating someone as an integral whole, as a person who has a right to nonoppressing choices over his or her own destiny and gives that right to others as long as their choices do not imply oppression.

2. *Don't do things that seem foolish to you,* but try to understand why people make ridiculous demands. Look upon your school as a small and barbaric society; that is, the teachers and administrators act to keep themselves in power. Make a list of the ways in which their actions and their words do not fit together. Become a participant—observe and study your school, so that if it ever comes down to a conflict, you know its strengths and weaknesses, and you know the behavior that makes your opponents most comfortable.

3. *Remember that though there may be a lot you haven't experienced or don't know, you are neither inferior nor stupid.* The school ruling class uses your own sense of inferiority against you, and it is just a political weapon, not a fact of nature. Self-hate and self-doubt keep competitive and inhumane schools running. If you believe you are inferior instead of understanding that you are oppressed, you will either turn out to be a good student or find yourself hating the badness, i.e., the defiance and sensibleness, in yourself.

4. *Initiate, initiate, initiate.* If your school is ugly, make it beautiful; begin many small programs and projects. Do not ask permission for everything you do. Focus on some specific things you and a few friends can change and want to change, and get to work quietly and quickly. Most of all, don't stand alone. Get to work with friends. Also, however, don't grow too big. A small collective, between four and twelve people, is generally much more effective and trusting than a large group.

Building allies is equally important for teachers. It is worth the time to hang out in the teachers' lunchroom and listen to other teachers as you would listen to your students. It also helps to notice who stays away from the teachers' lunchroom, for often these are the teachers who are fighting the system or putting in a little extra time getting things right in their classrooms or talking with students. These people have to be sought out, and so wandering the halls, peeking into rooms during lunchtime is as valuable as being in the teachers' room. And one can easily do both.

Asking for help is another way of making friends, building alliances, and making one's life in the classroom. Many young teachers are afraid to admit they are having trouble or that their ideas do not work automatically. Older teachers are often equally frustrated because no one asks for their advice. I have found that saying I'm having trouble teaching phonic blends or subtraction or the difference between a city and a state often brings out the most generous feelings on the part of teachers one might not otherwise have anything to do with. The more specific the questions, the more willing people are to help you and share the tricks they've picked up or developed.

For those teachers who you feel might become friends, the only way to know them at ease is away from school—over dinner or a beer. There is no harm inviting people out if no one asks you, and others may be as shy as you are. The new person in a social system usually feels most awkward and is always worrying about being judged. However, friendly aggressiveness has its rewards, and the worst that can happen is that the person you invite out says no.

So far I have spoken of secretaries, janitors, and students. One step above the secretaries, though not at all as powerful within the school, are the paraprofessionals—the teachers' aides and teaching assistants. Their power and effectiveness usually reside in their relations to parents, students, and other community people. Often they are very threatening to the teachers because they are close to many of the students and can teach them to read and write in noncoercive ways, though they have no credentials. They are often better teachers than the credentialed people they are supposed to defer to, and this sets up considerable tension within a staff. A student teacher or young teacher who consorts with the aides stands to learn a lot about the students, the community they live in, and the kind of learning situations they respond to. However, she or he also courts the hostility of the other teachers.

Being a teacher is being smack in the middle of the social system of the school. The students and nonprofessional adults are underneath, and the administrators and all the bureaucrats at the central district office, as well as the school board, are above. There is status to the role and a certain amount of power and independence within one's own classroom. However, the teacher is subject to demands from below and directives from above. A teacher who becomes too close to the students or nonprofessional staff is looked upon as subverting the social order, while one too close to the administration is considered a climber. However discontent most teachers might be with the social system as a whole, they obey certain rules in order to protect their status and maintain some solidarity as a group, no matter how much internal tension there might be among them. Some of the rules are:

1. Never criticize or disagree with another teacher in front of a student.
2. Never criticize another teacher at a faculty meeting with administrators present.
3. Never criticize another teacher to a parent.
4. When asked for an opinion at an open meeting, never say anything that might offend another teacher.
5. Pick your clique of teachers at the school, and eat lunch with them or alone in your room. Don't cross class lines to socialize in a way that is too apparent during school hours.
6. If a student appeals to you for protection against another teacher, always support the teacher in front of the student. If you must talk to the teacher, do it in private.

All of these rules serve to present a facade of unity among the staff before students and administrators. Young teachers who do not observe these rules are looked upon as potential radicals or troublemakers. I was transferred out of two schools—once for defending a student against another teacher in public, and once for criticizing a racist teacher openly at a staff meeting. The principal of each of those schools saw me as disruptive, as did most of the other teachers, and for the tranquillity of the community I had to go. In the first instance, defending the student, I would do it again and any time. If being a teacher means refusing to prevent young people from being brutalized, then it's not worth it. However, in criticizing the racist teacher, I think my words were ineffective. I left the school and the other teacher stayed. Perhaps if I'd been cooler, kept a record of his actions, established myself with the students and parents, belonged to a small cell of teachers ready to act, then the public confrontation might have had a different outcome. But I was too new at the school, struggling on too many fronts at once. My classroom was not together—I was just learning how to teach. The parents barely knew me; all the teachers were still looking me over, as was the principal.

New teachers must focus on their teaching and on figuring out the strengths and weaknesses of the social structure of their school, as well as identify their friends and enemies before they can take on the system. It is of no value to anyone to get wiped out too soon.

This does not mean it isn't possible to change things. In some cases there are administrators waiting for teachers to help them change their schools, to cross class lines, or eliminate them, in the service of the students and the community. In other instances, there are combinations of teachers, parents, and students that can be effective. There is no single way to go about changing a school. One must analyze every individual situation, assess strengths and weaknesses, keep documents, and date incidents that might be of use. One can move effectively in a situation only after one understands it.

Action based on practical analysis of a situation and informed by humanistic and equalitarian ideology is called praxis. Without this unification of analysis and theory, change rarely occurs, and many young teachers are wiped out before they can be effective.

At the top of the hierarchy on the school site is the principal and the other administrators who are supposed to support him or her. In most schools the role of the principal is to avoid bad publicity for the school. His or her prime job is not pedagogical or even managerial. It involves public relations and the avoidance of trouble. For this reason the principal is usually reluctant to support change within his or her school that might possibly lead to controversy. However, it also means that if enough pressure is brought to bear, the principal will usually yield a bit, if he or she feels that there is no way of wiping out the opposition. A good example of the kind of pressure that can be mobilized happened in Berkeley four years ago. Two teachers in one of the junior high schools wanted to have 100 students, three classrooms, and their own books and supplies within the context of the junior high. They did not want to start a private junior high, but rather have a semiautonomous public junior high that would be open and would involve student and parent governance, and yet would share the facilities and resources of the existing junior high.

The first time the teachers approached the principal with this idea, he looked at them as if they were mad. The idea was unheard of, what would the parents say, and how would the rest of the staff respond? He gave the teachers a thousand reasons why they couldn't have their minischool, though none of the reasons questioned the educational soundness of the ideas. The teachers were discouraged, but decided that they probably could get the school eventually if they started more modestly. They proposed to the principal the next day that they not have the school, but be allowed to develop an elective class for the next semester. The class was entitled Contemporary Education Theory. The teachers proposed a mini junior high based on open principles. The plan was broached to the parents, many of whom were definitely interested. They kept on meeting, and by the end of the school year a plan was developed, a proposal written, and community support mobilized. In June, the teachers approached the principal with their plans for a new school once again. However, this time they went to him with parents and students. He still opposed their plan, but this time he was more cautious since he was dealing with parents as well as teachers. He didn't exactly turn them down. He claimed that he didn't have the power to grant their request and sent them to the assistant superintendent, who also claimed he had no power to act, and sent them to the superintendent, who told them he would study the matter. The issue was almost filed away for several years by the superintendent in a slick, professional way. No one had been turned down, no one had been accepted, no battles and no public bitterness. However, the parents were not willing to quit. Moreover, they were angered at how powerless they were to effect even slow and responsible change. The step-by-step battle up the hierarchy was a form of political education for the parents and made them more committed to the minischool than before. At this point, the school was given a name, and the teachers and parents and students talked about it as if it already existed.

The parents went to the school board and requested action. They did not ask for any extra money and did not want to be put off by a feasibility study that would last a year. They wanted the school next September.

After the whole history of the planning and development of the school was presented, as well as the fact that the principal had allowed the elective course to happen, the board voted that the superintendent should find a way to make the school exist. By the next September, the school came into existence, and it still continues.

The teachers refused to accept the principal's no as a final determination of the matter. They tried every trick they could pull to get the necessary power to have their alternative. They were willing to battle over a long period of time, go through the hierarchy, and teach the elective for six months while continuing to teach other classes at the junior high that were repugnant to them. And in this rare case they won.

I think their ingenuity and persistence and the energy they put into educating the parents paid off in a way that a direct personal confrontation with the principal would not have. Of course, if the school board had said no, it would have been a different matter. Then the teachers would have had several options—try to close down the junior high and gain strength through confrontation in the streets; run a candidate in the next school board election or work on the school board members in private; have their own school without public money and continue to confront the school system with its own failure to respond to the needs and the demands of the community; go back into the school and subvert it; or, finally, to quit and go back to life as usual.

PLANNING CHANGE

When planning change in your school, there are a number of strategies that can be adopted. You can, of course, try to go it on your own. You can close your door to the rest of the school and try to make things as decent as possible for your students while they are with you. However, it is very hard to remain isolated within your school. An open, responsive classroom is often threatening to the other teachers at the school. They fear that it may turn the heads of their pupils and make control and discipline more difficult. In some ways these teachers' fears are justified.

Students who see, by the example of an open classroom in their school, that a sterile form of school life is not necessary may begin to demand that things change. Too often their defiance will be punished summarily. And the matter may not stop there. The innovative teacher may be blamed for his students' actions. And he, too, may meet with various subtle restraints.

Sooner or later, the teacher interested in opening things up will have to confront uptight teachers with his work and fight to make it possible for his type of teaching to exist within a public school setting. This is extremely difficult if the teacher is completely alone in a school.

There are other pitfalls in trying to develop an open classroom on one's own. As a teacher, you have to be constantly responding to the needs of individual students and getting resource material and people as well as developing your own ideas. Your students become hungry to learn, and the textbook will not provide fully for their needs.

When let go, students want to learn so many different things that it is almost impossible for any one adult to keep up with them. Many teachers fear that students will be lazy when allowed freedom. Actually, given the time and an atmosphere of trust, young people often want to learn more than educational theorists claim they are capable of learning.

You will face other problems in the confinement of a single classroom. At any given time there are different activities that students will be involved in. Some will require movement and noise, others the presence of music, and still others relative silence and solitude. If the classroom is to resemble life, all of these activities must be permitted to go on. The classroom should not be structured so that some forms of activity are permitted and others, usually the more spontaneous and physical, and the solitary ones, are prohibited. It is sensible to cluster quiet activities in one part of the room and even use the hall or closet if possible. Also, limits have to be set so that students learn to respect each other's work and style. There is nothing wrong with working with the radio on, but it is inconsiderate to turn the radio up so loud that other students can't function. Fitting a range of learning styles and a variety of activities into a classroom takes a lot of time and experimentation, especially at the beginning of the school year. However, learning to make the adjustments and compromises in order to live together genially is an important learning experience itself, one that can create a pleasant learning community.

It is also difficult to force upon young people the necessity of relating to one and only one adult during a school year. Some adults relate better with active rather than passive children. Others appreciate boys more than they do girls, or athletes instead of intellectuals. Students also have their preferences among adults. Within a single classroom, neither the adult nor the children have a choice. They must relate to each other, like it or not, and this often gives rise to conflicts that could have been avoided if the teachers and students had a choice of people to work with.

There is a final problem I would like to mention, one which has particularly distressed me. What happens if one succeeds in opening up the classroom and enabling students to pursue what they consider relevant and relate to you as a person and not as a teacher? What about the next year; what happens to the children if they pass back into a rigid, hostile situation where creativity and honesty will be looked upon as defiance? I do not think this is a valid reason for one to adopt an authoritarian posture, but it is a question to worry about.

None of these problems is so difficult if you are not alone. A while ago four of us worked together in an elementary school. We didn't talk much about our work with the rest of the faculty, and they didn't seem particularly interested. What we tried to do was get our rooms placed together at the end of a hall and then use the four rooms and the hall space as a separate school within our school. The students in the four classes were free to move from one room to another or use the hall as part of our minischool. It would have been ideal if there was a set of swinging doors that separated us from the rest of the building, or if we had been placed in four adjoining portable classrooms in a remote part of the school yard. But we did the best we could at one end of a long hallway.

We looked out for each other's students and tried to help each other out. I was concerned with writing, another teacher with athletics, a third with history and sociology, and the last with soul music. We just made a beginning and didn't realize the possibilities we had for creating an alternative open school within our existing school without having to ask anyone for extra money.

These days I am working with small groups of teachers, trying to develop open minischools within existing schools. I am sure it can be done, that all of us can do it, though not without hard work and resistance.

The first step is to sound out other teachers, asking them what they think about education in general. Broach the question of what they think about your school only after you have a general feeling that they may be discontented with the way things are.

Meet with interested teachers away from the school building. If you think it might help, give them material on open education you feel might move them along. Perhaps a pot-luck supper or a picnic would be a good occasion to begin discussions.

Once you have identified a few people it might be possible to work with, there are many ways to proceed, according to the nature of your school, the number of people interested, the kind of community support you are likely to get, and so forth.

Fundamental changes must arise out of the specific needs and problems of individual students and teachers. They cannot be packaged. Let me give a few examples of specific qualitative changes that can open things up and lead to the development of open minischools:

1. Spatial restructuring can take place by eliminating fixed and assigned seating in the classroom. On the first day of school let the students sit where they choose and let them change seats at will

throughout the year. Disputes about seating can be dealt with as practical problems to be solved by the persons involved rather than as discipline problems requiring punishment.

2. Temporal change can take place by abandoning the notion of spending fixed periods of time on individual subjects. Reading can go as long as people are involved in it; math can be forgotten for a few weeks and then returned to; history can take up a few weeks to the exclusion of other subjects and then be dropped for a while. More radically, punctuality could be given up as a moral concept. Students could come to school between 8 and 10 and leave any time from 2 to 4. If school is interesting, students will stay. If not, they ought not be confined.

3. You, the teacher, can give up the power to punish or grade students, can give up lecturing all the time, and instead spend time discovering interesting things to add to the classroom environment.

While these three types of innovation cost nothing financially, they do require a great deal of your time, work, and patience before they begin to work well. Once they take root, however, life in school just might be more fun and richer for everyone concerned.

An open school within an existing school probably has the best chance of succeeding if it starts from the ground up, from the teacher and the students who must live with it, and therefore it cannot be imposed from above. You cannot tell people, "Be open," and expect anything but a mockery of a free situation to develop.

Teachers and students who are interested in opening things up must start by considering how they can do it in their school with the specific conditions they face. For example, how many students are willing to try something new? How many supportive parents are around? How much support can be expected from the administration? From other teachers?

There are other specific questions to be considered: what part of the school is most isolated and will provide the minischool with the privacy it might need? How much cooperation will be gotten from janitors, school secretaries, parent aides, special teachers? You must estimate the strengths and weaknesses of your specific situation.

In some schools it is easiest to develop an experimental

program with "special" students whom the school has given up on. In other cases, all students are so ready for change that you would hardly know where to begin. You must spend time assessing the specific nature of your school in order to develop a strategy for change. It is not enough to have good ideas or good intentions.

I want to add a cautionary note: too many goodwilled attempts to change public schools are destroyed because the teachers and students involved believe that the rightness and humaneness of their ideas are sufficient to eliminate opposition and open things up. It doesn't usually work out that way. People in power do not like to give up their power, even though their positions may be intellectually and humanely untenable.

There are several general strategies that I would like to end with. They have been evolved by a number of people who have gone through the agonies of trying to restructure their public schools:

1. At the beginning, it is usually unwise to cut off completely people who claim to be interested in innovation and yet are not trusted or are not personal friends of members of the core group.
2. All reasonable objections to your plans must be met reasonably and patiently.
3. Plans ought to be kept out in the open.
4. The project needs to be open to intelligent evaluation.
5. If all these conditions are met and there is still serious opposition to change, you ought to be willing to go ahead anyway, even if it means taking risks.

KNOWING THE COMMUNITY

In order to succeed with any new program one needs the support of parents and other community people. They must understand what you are trying to do and be willing to fight alongside you. This is no easy matter since most teachers do not work at schools they attended as children. They are strangers, outsiders. Most of us do not even teach in communities we grew up in and belong to. Therefore, it is not surprising that knowing the community one's school serves can be a problem for the teachers.

This is especially true for middle-class teachers working in working-class communities or for teachers working in communities in which they are racial outsiders. A white teacher in a black or Chicano community, a Chicano teacher in a white or black community, an Asian teacher in a black community, a black teacher in an Asian community—all are outsiders who have to prove themselves.

There are many things people in a community will not tell a teacher about themselves. The teacher is an agent of authority, just like the policeman or social worker. His or her power is over the future of the child; failure in academics, bad conduct grades, referrals to guidance counselors are looked on as much in terms of their own future effects (my child won't get into college or get a good job) as their present meaning in the life of the child. Parents learn not to speak their minds in the presence of teachers, to defer to their professional judgments, and remain as neutral as possible. Earnest young teachers who want to know about the community in order to help the children are treated as coldly as the most indifferent teachers. Trust in a community is established through crisis or common battle. When a child is threatened with suspension and a teacher supports the child and risks the principal's disapproval, trust develops. When a teacher gives his or her own time to work with students having trouble, helps students not in his or her own class, talks to probation officers, gets to know families instead of individuals and takes political and personal risks with them, then trust develops. However, this takes years, and one must get by with a partial knowledge of the community at the beginning. The way this knowledge develops is of crucial importance in determining how the teacher builds a program for his or her students.

For example, it is not unusual for teachers to look at a poor community using what could be called a deficiency model. They look to see what their students do not know or do not experience or do not own. They measure their students' lives, and those of their students' families, by the standards of middle-class professional life. This negative set is almost moral in tone—teachers call their students disadvantaged, say their language is deficient, their experience limited, their exposure minimal. It is easy to slip from this mode of thinking into conceiving your role as teacher as a completely remedial one. The children can be looked at as coming to school disadvantaged, unable to learn sophisticated things, needing to be treated as if they were slightly retarded. These attitudes frequently develop without a teacher ever having spent time with parents and their children, without any real idea of what their students' lives are like twenty-four hours a day, seven days a week.

This picture may seem like a caricature, yet in a recent issue of the *National Elementary Principal,* the official journal of the National Association of Elementary School Principals, Scott, Foresman ran the following ad for its new reading system under a picture of a middle-aged white teacher walking up the stairs of an old school:

> "You know what I like? I like a reading program that can really get children ready to read. For example, some of our children need a lot of what I call *language* work. They come to us without much background in the concepts and experiences beginning reading is built on. I don't think anyone ever talked with them much about colors or animals or things they like and don't like. These children need to listen carefully, to talk a lot, to have stories read to them.
>
> "We have to give these children language-development experiences before we begin to teach them to read."

There is another way to look at a community or, more specifically, at what one's students bring with them to school. This could be called the strength model. Instead of looking for deficiencies, one can ask: what strengths do my students bring with them to school? More specifically, one can ask, and then find a way to answer:

1. What games do my students already know?
2. What church experiences have they had? How much do they know about the Bible?
3. What have they learned from older brothers and sisters?
4. Who are the heroes in the neighborhood?
5. Where do the students go shopping?
6. What do they know about money? Many students can add, subtract, multiply, and divide with money, but are confused when the teacher talks about apples and balls.

7. What language games do the children like to play? What kind of insults and praises do they use?
8. What words are they exposed to every day in the neighborhood? On billboards? In store windows? Scrawled on the walls?
9. Where did the children's families come from? Where do the children vacation in the summer?
10. What kind of cars, minibikes, motorcycles, and bikes do they use? Admire? Know how to fix?
11. What music do they listen to? What does it say? Do they invent their own music? Play instruments?
12. What dances do they do? How do they learn them?
13. Where do they go on special occasions? Where do their parents go? What clubs do they belong to?
14. Who are their favorite entertainers?
15. Who is their oldest living relative? What does he or she remember of the past?
16. What does each child enjoy doing most? What is his or her particular genius?

This list could continue indefinitely. The positive strengths of self and culture provide more than enough material and understanding for teachers to build a curriculum that is continuous with the rest of the lives of their pupils and challenges them to grow as fully as possible. The strength model can also provide the knowledge to allow oneself to act in the service of the community and make allies in whatever educational struggles one undertakes.

SUSTAINING CHANGE

Often it will be possible to mobilize energy and have an opportunity to develop a minischool or even control a whole school. However, merely being able to develop a program based on a new way of working with young people does not guarantee that you will be able to do what you hope. The struggle to make a decent learning place is often more difficult than the struggle one has to go through in order to be able to attempt it.

There are a number of problems that have been experienced by people developing new schools and they are worth thinking about. A first important consideration for any program is how it is initiated. Some of the new schools I observed were initiated by the principal and others by a small group of teachers (usually from three to five).

The new schools that were developed by administrative decree usually had serious problems. The participating teachers didn't know why they were there and didn't particularly see a need for an open alternative in their school. They felt it was just another idea the principal had picked up from a book. These new schools developed by administrative decree hardly differed from regular schools, and the students seemed bored.

New schools that were initiated by teachers, but without administrative support, had different problems. They had pressure from all sides—from other teachers, from supervisors, and often from parents who spoke to the supervisors. However, these schools were holding their own, primarily because of the teachers' personal commitments to openness and change. I felt that the students in these schools considered themselves a part of an important, though pressurized, experiment.

The new schools that seemed to function most smoothly were those that were initiated by teachers and that had some administrative protection. In these schools, the teachers were left alone to develop their ideas and to create a comfortable environment for their children. The administrators protected them from the complaints of other teachers and from the uneasiness of some parents.

These last schools usually had another characteristic: they had been given several years' grace by the administrators. The new schools that were declared one-year experiments were in bad shape. The pressure of having to produce in one year was just too much for some of these schools. I know from my own experience that it takes at least three years to develop an open learning environment.

There is another problem that has to do with the way in which new schools are set up. Some teachers think of open schooling as relevant only for "difficult" students and, therefore, develop their schools accordingly. There is, of course, one advantage to this situation: other teachers are more likely to be cooperative if you agree to take the "difficult" children off their hands.

This advantage, however, is far outweighed by the disadvantage of being the safety valve for the rest of the school. There are four reasons for this:

First, the students within the new school are often stigmatized as dumb or retarded by the other students and teachers.

Second, the student population constantly changes as new "difficult" students emerge during the course of the school year. The new school community never has a chance to settle down.

Third, the open school is not a psychotherapeutic environment, even though it is therapeutic in the sense that children can function and grow in a healthy situation where they are respected as individuals. Teachers in open schools are not therapists and cannot deal with severe problems, nor should they consider themselves the saviors of all students.

Fourth, if a new school hopes to have an impact on the rest of the school, it must convince everyone that it is a real alternative for *all* of the people in the school and not just for those who are characterized as troublesome. At Other Ways, a new school where I worked a few years ago, we considered ourselves an alternative school whose students represented a cross section of the children in the Berkeley Unified School District. We were not a safety valve for the rest of the system.

A second group of major problems that new schools run into involves the relationships among the adults working in the school. By and large, teachers are not accustomed to working together with a large group of children. They are used to having *their* class and *their* students. They are also unaccustomed to the constant presence of other adults in the classroom. But in open schools, the teachers work with each other, sharing information and resources and giving up their solitary power over the school lives of their children.

New-school teachers I have spoken to say that a lot of meetings are necessary for the teachers to get to know each other. The meetings are usually held in the relaxed and informal atmosphere of a staff member's house, rather than at school. Most of the teachers in the new schools that seem to be doing well like each other and spend a lot of time together socially.

Obviously, a lot of adjustment within the adult community is necessary to achieve this harmonious state of affairs. Teachers must be able to take criticism and give it—out of love and concern rather than out of anger and hatred. This give-and-take atmosphere was strikingly evident in the successful new schools I visited; members of the original groups who felt uncomfortable with the direction the new school was taking had been given the option to leave.

Each new-school has had to develop some means by which the teachers can deal with problems as they occur. Some of the schools brought in outside experts in group processes to conduct a criticism group for the whole staff. Other schools developed their own self-criticism groups; still others made sure that they brought in the students during the staff meetings.

Getting the teachers to work together harmoniously is no easy matter, and there is no single method guaranteed to achieve it. It is, however, a prerequisite for the development of a successful open school.

A third class of problems has to do with centering the new school around some concern or problem, project or place. In order to become a community, the new schools must develop ties that bind the students and teachers together. Yet at the same time sufficient diversity must be maintained so that many different styles and interests are accommodated.

In some schools, a student-teacher lounge with a record player, records, chess sets, magazines, and books provides a center for the school. In others, it is a shop that is also a reading lab, or a kitchen where the children and teachers take turns preparing food. One school leased some land, and the children and teachers designed, built, and used some geodesic domes.

New schools can also be oriented around the development of knowledge of the local community, around ecology, around the relationships between art and technology, around the making and using of books, around psychological studies—in fact, around almost everything that involves the majority of students and teachers in the new school without compelling them to be involved.

The quest for an identity for the new school is a real problem that takes time and effort to solve. However, identity can come in a most unexpected way. For example, our school went on a retreat. During our time in the country, the question of survival in the wilderness arose. After the trip, we created a wilderness survival class. One child suggested that we also have an urban survival class. Out of these two classes grew the idea of looking at all the things we were doing in the light of their contribution to human survival. This became the theme through which our school developed an identity.

I think the quest for identity has been the major problem of the first year's existence of all the new schools I have seen. Once a theme emerges or a common problem develops, other problems have a way of disappearing. Awareness of the need for a center for the new school can contribute to finding one.

THE SCHOOL BOARD

It is important to know about the community politics that determine school board policy. The closer you can get to the members of the school board, the more likely it is that the professional administration will lay off you or accept changes you initiate.

School boards are appointed or elected. In either case, the people comprising the board usually are not educators and do not pretend to know how to teach youngsters. They have a vague sense of what they would like to see happening in the schools and a clearer sense of what they do not want to see. They usually delegate to the superintendent and his staff the entire business of carrying out their policies and handling questions of teaching styles and school organization. Consequently, in all but a few communities the superintendent and his staff effectively control education in the community, with the exception of socially and politically charged issues like integration, sex education, and so forth.

These conditions exist partially because very few communities support their school board members on a full-time basis. In Berkeley, for example, each board member receives five dollars a meeting. Unless one is independently wealthy, it is impossible to be a full-time board member and know what is actually going on in the schools. The superintendent has to be counted upon to educate the board, and he will tell them what he chooses.

These circumstances can be both advantageous and disadvantageous. An ignorant school board can be more easily educated about issues of learning and teaching than a professional board that believes it knows everything. Furthermore, a board that has been deceived into believing that everything is all right can be taken to the schools and shown what is actually happening. It can be exposed to the children and the parents. Since the board is political, it will respond to community pressure in ways that rigid professionals will not.

Furthermore, being political, the board members are used to wheeling and dealing. If they have favorite programs, they will protect them. I have found that a single board member who can be persuaded to take up open education and develop and protect some educational alternatives can be more helpful than a whole board that is only partially convinced. A lot of effort should go into finding one or two board members and educating them thoroughly.

Assume that the members of your school board do not know much about learning and about alternatives to the formal classroom. Take it upon yourself to educate them. First of all, buy them some paperback books like *How Children Fail* and *The Lives Of Children* (it is more effective to give people books than a reading list that can be dumped into a wastebasket), as well as a book on English informal education. They might at least read the jacket copy and at best the books and become interested in learning.

Also do a fact sheet on the school district to provide the board with useful information. For example, tell them about the number of dropouts, about the number of students taking drugs or assigned to classes for the disturbed. Give them a list of all the building violations of the public school facilities; find out about ways in which the administration wastes money and document them. This requires that you research your own community (see the section entitled "Knowing the Community") and present what could be called a radical social and fiscal analysis of conditions in the local schools.

Also, give the board a clear and nonjargonese paper on what you hope to do to change the schools. Try to move them—give them case histories, specifics, photos of what open classrooms and schools look like. Get them to depend as little as possible on their imaginations, which will probably conjure up pictures of chaos, which threatens them, and which in any case is a problem for their psyches and not for your alternative program.

Make a case to the board that alternatives are not expensive because they depend for the most part on different structures and attitudes rather than upon more expensive objects or facilities. Money is an obsession with school boards, and anything that does not sound expensive is of interest.

Recently, I talked to a member of County Board of Education who had been told about open schooling and was curious to learn more. He knew that the kids were dropping out even in that rural farm community. He was aware that there were growing problems with the Chicano population, which was beginning to organize. However, he also knew that the schools were almost broke, and that his community would not yet tolerate alternatives that were presented with radical rhetoric. He asked me a series of questions that I think people who are trying to move a school board will have to respond to:

1. How much does it cost to run an alternative school, both in the short run and over a long period of time? And how does this cost compare to what is now being spent in the schools in this particular community?
2. How can the community be convinced to accept alternatives? Here it is possible to give the board member some arguments. An open school is not that much different from a good one-room schoolhouse. An alternative school tries to involve as many people from the community as possible, including older people who presently feel unconnected. It is possible to use many work facilities in the community as learning places for the young, and therefore to bring the young and old together.
3. What kind of facilities are necessary? There are many answers to this since alternative schools can exist anywhere, from people's apartments to storefronts to domes set up on vacant land to sections of existing schools. Many people equate school with large, prisonlike buildings, and alternative locations will frequently come as a surprise. For this reason it is a good idea to pick some specific locations in your community that might be good places for schools, such as old supermarkets and factories, to show to the board. It also would probably help to tell the board that the same amount they pay to lease portable classrooms can be used to bring old structures

up to school code and also that the rent on portables is a continuing expense, while bringing the building up to code need only happen once. Over a period of five years, a renovated factory is cheaper than a portable classroom. This is also a good response to question number 1.

4. How does one start an alternative school?
5. How can the board and the parents tell if the alternative school is working and how much time should it be given to prove itself?

In those communities where there is an elected school board, it makes sense to find someone who supports alternative education and convince him or her to run in the next election. Most school board elections are popularity contests. Those that aren't are usually run on politically and socially charged issues like integration or the use of sex education in the schools. Very few elections ever deal with the way in which the schools should be structured or the choices of learning styles and teachers available to students and parents. School board elections usually do not deal with fundamental issues of teaching and learning.

Most of the people who enter elections want to win. However, it makes sense to run an educational campaign whose major goal is to convince people in the community that alternative schooling presents a sensible way to deal with the school problems of the young of the community. For an educational campaign it is important to choose a candidate who will be listened to in the part of the community you want to reach. In Berkeley these days people feel a need to have public offices occupied by women and Third-World people, so a sensible candidate would be a Third-World woman who can present educational alternatives. If a student community is to be reached, a student makes sense, and if a street community, a street person might be a sensible choice. The crucial thing is that the candidate be heard and that the candidate and those people behind the candidate put out all sorts of documents dealing with the schools.

Student communities are particularly ripe for school board elections. Usually these elections have small turnouts, and if students can be mobilized to ring doorbells and talk to people, and to vote themselves, a political force for alternative schooling can develop.

A campaign of this sort can be considered successful if it creates a sense within the community that there are voters who are willing to support alternative schooling, and that all the school board candidates had better start thinking about educational issues. The campaign can serve to educate the other candidates for the board, as well as the rest of the community, and then after the election the board can be approached to support alternatives, whether or not the election has been won.

A group of people including John Hurst, a professor at the University of California School of Education, Joan Levinson, a teacher at Bay High School, and I, all of whom were involved in alternative schools both inside and outside the public school system, decided to run one of our people for the Berkeley School Board. Joan was chosen because: (1) she was articulate, (2) she worked in an alternative school, (3) she was known in the community, and (4) she was a woman. The people that supported Joan set themselves up as the New Schools Network and tried to bring in as many people as possible who were concerned with alternative education. We sponsored a few benefits and films and set up cocktail parties and small pot-luck dinners, as well as a telephone chain. Students in the existing alternative schools knocked on people's doors and tried to explain what alternative schools were. John Hurst mobilized some students from the university in Berkeley, and they did artwork and manned telephones as well as talked up the school board election on campus.

The Network decided to flood the community with information about alternative schools. Several posters were printed and displayed throughout the community, and an endorsement was gotten from our congressman, Ronald Dellums. Three white papers were printed and distributed free throughout the community. (These papers and the campaign platforms are included at the end of this section.) A logo was created, and buttons and bumper stickers were printed. We used the underground presses and got small contributions to support the campaign. John Holt and Jim Herndon came to talk (it makes sense to ask local educational celebrities to speak to bring out the people to meet the candidate). Joan spoke at all of the candidates' endorsement meetings, hitting on the issue of alternative schooling. She appeared before the Democrats, Republicans, and Radicals, before the chamber of commerce, the manufacturers associations, and all other groups that endorsed school board candidates.

By the time the campaign ended, Joan had gotten all of the other candidates to respond publicly to the issue of alternative schools. Joan received 13,135 votes and came in fourth out of a field of fifteen. The first three candidates were elected. However, a constituency for alternative education was established and its spokespeople, who were active in Joan's campaign, have continued to have an effect on school board policy.

Modesto is quite different from Berkeley. It is an agricultural town in the San Fernando Valley and is very conservative. In the town there is little large industry, no major university, and a large, though not well-organized, Chicano community. The school board is conservative and not responsive to the Chicano population or the few town liberals and radicals.

The only large industrial facility is the Shell Oil Agronomical Research Center, which employs many biologists and chemists with doctorates and masters degrees. Many of the young scientists are hip and consider themselves to be somewhat radical. There is also a local junior college, and several faculty members are interested in changing the schools.

Several years ago I was involved in a teacher training program for the Modesto public schools. At that time I met a small group of teachers and parents who wanted to create an alternative school within the Modesto school system. With a little encouragement they set up a group called Parents for Alternative Schools and set out to educate the community about alternative education and build local support. They got a professor at the local junior college to sponsor an extension course on alternative education, which was used as a respectable base for them to organize. The parents and teachers in the course visited functioning alternative and free schools, including the school I then taught at, and began to make plans to approach the school board. The superintendent said he was interested, but claimed that he could not act without board sanction.

At that time the school board elections were coming up, and one of the members of the group, Art Henry, decided to run for the board with the specific intent of educating the community about alternative schools and creating the climate where they would be accepted.

Art has two sons in the public schools and is a biochemist at Shell. He is also somewhat radical for the Modesto community, but is respected because he has a Ph.D., a house, and an intact family. In other words, he is a parent, a property owner, and a taxpayer.

Art ran a campaign similar to Joan's, except that it was geared to the community of Modesto rather than to Berkeley. He printed posters and flyers, made buttons and bumper stickers. He went to all of the candidates' nights and had parties and pot-luck dinners and receptions. Many people told him that he was crazy to run and that he had no chance of winning. However, winning was not the issue—the issue was educating the community, and in that Art succeeded. He received 3,000 votes and came out way down at the bottom of the list of candidates. But alternative schools emerged as a live and sensible public issue. And the Parents for Alternative Schools picked up several hundred members. The group went to the board several times after the election and has at present a modest alternative school supported by the public school system and run by the parent group. And that is just a beginning.

I have also heard that many people in situations similar to Art's in other valley towns like Stockton and Merced looked at the campaign and its results very carefully and have begun to do their own work. Within its limited goals, Art's campaign must certainly be considered a success. However, it is a success that cannot be considered an end in itself. It is just the beginning of years of work that might lead to many educational alternatives in the community. The danger is that people will take that modest victory as an ultimate effort and feel that there is no more fighting to be done. What was gained can easily be wiped away unless the battle is continued.

Here is a copy of the platform we wrote for the Berkeley election:

> The recently revealed crisis in the Berkeley school budget and the concurrent school board elections could be one of the best things

that has happened in many years. For the money problem is forcing us to take a hard look at our schools and just what it is we want them to be.

The Berkeley community supports its schools generously—this year about $1700 will be spent on each student. And Berkeley can be justifiably proud that it was the first city to achieve racially integrated schools. But money and integration do not automatically make good schools.

Many students still feel imprisoned, bored, and angry. Black parents still see a six-year lag in their children's reading levels compared with white students'.

Some students feel they cannot really concentrate on academic learning in the present situation; others want a freer atmosphere in which to develop. Perhaps the single most striking statistic in the whole picture is the fact that Berkeley High's average full-day attendance rate is only 50 percent!

Berkeley's children are marvelously varied and highly sophisticated. We need schools that fit them. That means schools in which the students and teachers and parents have increasing responsibility for what happens. There are many ways to grow and many places in which to learn. Teachers have ideas and talents and interests that need to be encouraged. Parents can contribute skills and ideas and time. The community is rich in people, places, and events, all of which are educational and should be easily available to its younger members.

Recognizing the validity of this approach, the Board recently unanimously passed a resolution stating that the Berkeley District shall be a system of many schools.

We therefore propose:

That the whole school system be refashioned into small, autonomous schools, using the existing buildings, each school with its own budget. These sub-schools would reflect different styles and have different emphases, including traditional classrooms, skill centers, ethnic schools, experimental structures, academic schools, arts and science centers, apprenticeship arrangements, and *any others* that teachers and students and parents might want.

These are not impractical dreams. The Superintendent's office has evidence that existing sub-schools cost considerably less— between $800 and $1200 per student. The lower costs are mainly due to the reduced need for administration in a small school.

That students take gradually increasing responsibility for directing their own education. Our goal is that each child shall become a continuously growing, self-confident, autonomous person.

That the entire community be considered as a learning resource to be used by all children, with the schools serving as one of the main learning centers.

In addition to this document, we developed position papers on such topics as standardized tests, sex roles in the school, and integration. One of the papers was entitled "Positive Steps to Better Schools," and is reprinted below.

Positive Steps to Better Schools
In Support of Joan Levinson for School Board

Most kids don't like school. They simply endure it. Or they just don't go—in Berkeley High School the truancy rate is 50 percent. Teachers are dissatisfied and discouraged with the schools, as witness the recent upheavals among teachers' unions and the vote of no-confidence. And then there are the thousands of frustrated parents and taxpayers, who are supplying the $27 million spent annually on Berkeley schools, apparently without proportionate results. What's wrong? Where can we begin to make significant changes? Is it even possible to have schools that children are eager to return to, where teachers aren't exhausting themselves in efforts to keep kids silent and in their seats? Do such schools exist? YES. They are called alternative schools (also free schools, new schools), because they offer alternatives to the existing uniform and regimented schools. The New Schools Network is an open group of parents, teachers, and other persons interested in supporting the existing alternative schools, aiding in establishing new ones, and effecting changes in the Berkeley school system through Joan Levinson, their candidate for the School Board. As their representative on the Board, what exactly would she do?

1. *Hold school-by-school hearings on alternative programs,* to find out what the faculty and/or parents would like to offer. The Board or a subcommittee would go to each school and ask the community to come out with their suggestions, skills, and ideas.

Such alternative programs would make more efficient use of internal school resources by:

a.   discovering what teachers already in the district like to do and could teach in order to broaden the range of choices available to students
b.   making existing resources (equipment, vehicles, facilities) more directly available to teachers and students in the district.

Alternative programs would also mean a more efficient use of external resources by:

a.   integrating the skills of tradesmen and craftsmen into the schools
b.   moving classroom activities into the community whenever and wherever possible.

2. *Establish alternative classrooms in every school in the district.* Teachers already at a school would be encouraged to develop alternative programs, with the help of people already working in such classrooms, if they wish. Parents would be informed of the plans and would be involved in the development of the programs. Every attempt would be made to involve the local community in such alternatives. They might range from a two-teacher unit (shared room/hall learning centers) to a model that involves half an existing school.
3. *Make schools 24-hour facilities available to and part of the community in which they exist.* Creative low-cost redesigning of playgrounds could turn them into focal centers for neighborhood kids seven days a week.
4. *Survey all existing alternative programs and schools and inform people of them.*
5. *Survey the programs that are at present outside the school system and yet are serving "rejects" of the system.* See how they could be brought under the umbrella of the school system by developing a formula for a modified voucher plan. Set up guidelines for accountability that could be used for such programs.
6. *Develop guidelines for evaluating and implementing joint innovative projects among teachers, parents, and students,* and encourage people to take advantage of them. Develop forms of control, and

define the latitude of freedom necessary.

7. *Redefine the role of the School Board.* The Board sets policy, but how much can really be implemented if changes in policy are merely stated, and then left to professional administrators and supervisors to carry out? We need ways in which the Board can hold its employees accountable for executing the changes which new policies will require.

8. Finally, all of these innovations would and CAN be done within the framework of the state education codes.

Naturally the language used to move the Modesto community was not the same as that used in Berkeley:

Platform—Art Henry for Modesto School Board

There are many ways for a child to grow, many ways to learn. The ways offered by Modesto's schools don't satisfy all parents, students, and teachers. These people need alternatives. But even for those who are satisfied, there may be alternative ways of education of which they are unaware. The present schools are one alternative. Other alternatives can exist within the Modesto school system at the same time.

What Are Alternative Schools?

They are schools in which teachers, parents, and students work together in a *truly democratic manner* to design studies which they feel are educationally valuable. They can be the ones we have today. Or, they can also be skill centers, ethnic schools, experimental structures, academic schools, arts and science centers, apprenticeships, *whatever* teachers, parents, and students want.

What Advantage Do They Offer the Student?

Students take a gradually increasing responsibility for directing their own education. We believe a child can see his needs, interests, talents and can seek meaningful knowledge based on these qualities. A child who can make choices that guide his learning is more likely to stay in school, become involved, grow as a person, become self-confident, self-reliant. He comes to know himself in the alternative school.

What About Teachers?

Teachers have ideas, skills, interests which need to be encouraged, not squashed by rigid methods. In the alternative school, teachers' responsibility for education policies increases; their individual natures surface; they become free to create a learning situation as the professionals they are.

And Parents?

Parents become more than mere revenue sources. They can contribute their ideas, skills, time. Modesto is rich in people, places, events, natural history: all educational. Our children should have access to them through our schools. *These schools are also cheaper.* Much work of high-salaried administrators is handled by teachers, students, and parents.

Will It Work?

Systems such as we describe are operating all across the country. In California alone more than sixty communities have at least one such institution. WHY NOT MODESTO?

TEACHER ORGANIZATIONS AND STRIKES

There are two major teachers' organizations represented in most school districts. One of the organizations, usually called a Teachers Association, is affiliated with the National Education Association (NEA). The other, which is usually called a Teachers Federation, is affiliated with the American Federation of Teachers (AFT) and through it with the AFL-CIO.

Teachers Associations tend to be stronger in rural or small city communities. They have traditionally considered themselves "professional" organizations modeled somewhat after the American Medical Association. The American Federation of Teachers considers itself a union and not a professional association. It is most dominant in urban areas like New York and Chicago.

For many years the Teachers Associations were rather conser-

vative educationally. More recently, it is becoming difficult to tell
the organizations apart in terms of educational philosophy. Both
the Teachers Federations and the Teachers Associations are
dominated by traditional teachers and have within them smaller
caucuses of individuals who advocate open education. There also
are small groups within each organization that are politically
radical. However, it is important to realize that even within the
group of politically left teachers there are many disagreements on
educational philosophy.

The NEA and the AFT are struggling for power these days. In
states like California, where a collective bargaining law exists, they
face each other in local elections to determine which group will be
the sole bargaining agent for the district. In these organizational
struggles the main issues are teacher salaries and benefits, and job
protection. In order to win as large a following as possible the
organizations avoid taking any bold educational positions. This is
especially true on a state and national level within the organizations. Locals in different cities can develop different priorities, and
some often find themselves at odds with the local and national
organizations. It is crucial to understand, if you get involved in
teachers' organization politics, that if you try to make too many
changes or upset too many people, you will get pressure from the
state and national organizations.

Over the past fifteen years I've been in and out of the teachers'
union a number of times. In 1961, I joined the United Federation
of Teachers in New York City. At that time there were about 5,000
members in the organization. At my school there were four
teachers in the chapter. The rest of the staff either belonged to an
NEA affiliate or didn't believe in teachers organizing at all. At
union meetings we spent most of our time talking about educational issues—about reading programs, reorganizing the school,
sharing materials and teaching ideas, and so forth. That year we
went out on strike. I believe that was the first teachers' strike in
New York City, and the union won the strike quickly. Teachers got
across-the-board raises of $1,000, extra money for college credits
beyond the B.A., and increased benefits. Educationally nothing was
won or even fought for by the union leadership. However, the
union got a dues check-off, which meant that union dues could

simply be taken out of one's salary. Nobody had to go around
urging teachers to pay their dues as we had to do before the dues
check-off. The staff at our school, grateful for the raise that was
won by the strike, all signed up for membership. The meeting after
the strike the whole leadership of our chapter changed. We four
original union members were the radicals who initiated a good
thing but were no longer necessary and got voted out as delegates.
The same thing happened throughout the city. Union membership
went from around 5,000 to around 35,000, and many of the more
radical delegates as well as those concerned primarily with
educational issues were voted out.

I kept my union membership for several years despite those
changes. However, in 1966, I quit in disgust over the union's
position against community control of schools in Harlem and the
Ocean Hill–Brownsville area of Brooklyn. I knew the schools and
parents involved in the struggle in Harlem. The students in the
schools couldn't read or write. Most of the teachers hated their
work and couldn't stand being around the students. Parents at the
school moved to take over the schools out of despair. The union's
whole response was to protect any teacher, no matter how
incompetent, and to discredit the parents. There were rumors, for
example, that the parents were anti-Semitic. But a number of
Jewish teachers, myself included, believed that the parents were
right and crossed the picket lines and worked as hard as we could
to develop community control of the schools.

I do not believe in being blindly loyal to organizations or in
supporting any strike no matter what the reason for it. Working
people should and must organize to protect their rights and to
humanize their work. But if people strike for racist reasons, or to
cover up their own incompetence, or to take power away from
poorer people, I believe these strikes should be opposed.

There are times, however, when there are just reasons to go on
strike, and one has to be prepared to take the risks involved in
opposing public institutions like the school systems.

The day before school began last year the teachers in Berkeley
voted overwhelmingly for a strike. There is no single bargaining
agent for Berkeley teachers, yet about 40 percent belong to the
union, 40 percent to an NEA affiliate, and 20 percent are

independent. Together with a representative of the school counselors and psychologists, they form a Certificated Employees
Council, which conducts negotiations with the administration and
school board. This was the first time that all groups had agreed on
a strike, and on the first day of school over 95 percent of the
district's certificate staff stayed out.

The background to the strike was as follows: on April 15, 1975,
an agreement was reached for the next school year after four
months of negotiations. There was to be no raise. Salaries and
benefits were to be maintained, as well as limits on classroom size
and grievance procedures that had been worked out with the
administration over the past few years. However, on June 28, the
school board, declaring a fiscal emergency, unilaterally rescinded
the agreement, which is possible under California state law. They
announced a 2.5 percent salary cut and over a 2 percent cut in
benefits. In addition, they eliminated class-size maximums and
instituted a policy of transferring teachers from school to school
without prior notice or hearings. This last policy was implemented
over the summer so that a number of teachers returned from
vacation to find themselves at new schools.

Many of the teachers I spoke to did not believe in strikes. They
never imagined themselves on picket lines, and it was not money
that brought so many out. They felt they had been treated
arrogantly and inconsiderately and that their dignity had been
damaged.

All the teachers at Hillside School, where I have worked and
where my three children go to school, went on strike. None had
ever been on a picket line before, and for some the decision to
strike was not made until the night before the strike began. I, with
many parents and former teachers, came out that first day of the
strike to help and to let the picketers know they were not alone in
their struggle.

It was awkward that morning. People didn't know whether to
carry signs or not. They were uncertain about how to act toward
the principal, who is popular with the staff, and the school
secretary and custodian, both of whom are liked and respected.
Fortunately, the principal arrived early that day and had a chance
to talk to the picket captains and a few of the other teachers. He

had to cross the line or lose his job, and none of the teachers wanted him forced out. It was decided to support him in crossing the line for the sake of the school after the strike. At other schools, where the principal was not as popular or the teachers were angrier, it was more difficult for the administrators.

The same consideration was shown to the custodian, bus driver, and school secretary, all of whom expressed overt sympathy with the strike but whose jobs were threatened. Over the course of the strike, the secretary stayed out in support of the strike for one day, as did the custodian. The bus driver, along with her colleagues, published a letter of support in our local newspaper. They had all done as much as they felt they could to help the teachers since their organizations did not vote to strike.

A major problem was deciding how to respond to substitutes from outside the district who had been offered fifty dollars a day to cross the picket line. The teachers felt they could not afford to be lenient about this, and eventually a number of strategies were used. Some subs were talked into leaving. Others were either given a silent treatment or informed that they would be denied future work in Berkeley and other districts. A list of their names was posted outside the school. There was no violence, but the extreme anger that the teachers felt came out in various ways. In response, the district began to rotate subs from school to school.

When parents came to school, it was important to meet them and to discuss the issues. We chose to have teachers talk to those parents they knew best and could reach most easily. For people with day-care needs alternatives were provided by other parents as well as some of the teachers.

During the second week of the strike, it became apparent that though they refused to give in, some teachers did not feel comfortable on the picket line. The picketers talked to each other, supported each other, and tried to keep anxieties down.

The teachers had to find ways to keep their time occupied. Several decided to devote their nonpicketing time to child care centers in different parts of the community or to support strikers at schools that weren't as unified as Hillside. One teacher, Dan Peletz, composed songs for the strike and took his guitar from school to school, singing them. In all the years I have been with Hillside I have never seen the staff so warm and supportive toward each other.

There were continually a number of anxieties lurking in the teachers' minds. Would someone try to cross the line? How could you deal with a member of your own staff who tried to break the strike? There were schools in the district where some teachers did go in, and there were feelings of bitterness. Old friendships were wrecked; there was harassment, shouts of "scab."

Of course, there was also the financial anxiety and the fear of being fired. The school board tried to play on all of these anxieties as well as to pit the teachers' organizations against each other. Solidarity was crucial.

One thing came out clearly: strength under the pressure of a strike did not depend on age, teaching style, or the organization one belonged to. A factor that did seem to have an effect on the teachers' attitudes was their own family background. Those who came from working-class backgrounds and had seen parents and relatives on strike in the past showed the others how to act. This shifting of traditional patterns caused people who had never paid attention to one another or thought they had nothing to learn from each other to begin to communicate.

The strike lasted for six weeks. Then an arbitration committee was agreed upon, and the teachers went back to work pending a final agreement. The committee returned a report which restored only a part of what had been taken away from the teachers. However, the teachers were too tired and demoralized to go back out on strike; they weren't confident in their leadership, which had assured them that the committee would return a report favorable to the teachers. They voted to accept the committee report at the same time that the school board warned that next year teachers would have to be fired. Clearly, the teachers in Berkeley will have to face the issue of going out again.

The situation is not unique to Berkeley. Many of us will have to face the possibility of being on the picket line in the next few years, and it is important to share experiences. Perhaps the best way to conclude this discussion is to quote Dan Peletz, who described some of his experiences and reactions this way:

It is necessary to figure out some guidelines for my own behavior in a highly unusual situation. For the most part, I continue to rely on those values that govern my behavior during more normal circumstances. I don't intentionally harass people when there's no strike on, and I'm not intentionally harassing anyone now. I don't make a practice of calling people names, and I haven't started. I would not in any way hassle another regular staff member who decided to go into school. I respect each person's right to make his or her own decision, and a decision to go in must be a very painful one, indeed.

I wrote three or four songs and shared them, and if they offend, so be it. I stayed as honest as I know how to be in writing them, and I'll stand by them. My anger and frustration needed a vent, and I chose to write songs.

I've spent a lot of time talking to friends all over the district, many of whom I haven't seen in ages. And one of the great benefits of the strike is that every staff member on the line is feeling a great sense of connectedness, that somehow we all relate to one another and are all in the same boat.

Where do we go from here? This level of tension cannot be maintained, a fact which is obvious to everyone. Either we go back to work and admit defeat (which few people I talk to have any intention of doing) or the struggle will be escalated. It's all very new, but I feel good about what we're doing, I'm proud to stand up for what I believe, and I'm confident we will prevail.

AFTERWORD

AT THE END of this book I would like to reaffirm what was said in the introduction: teaching is a difficult craft to master and takes time and effort and energy and intelligence and feeling. It is easy to be seduced into concentrating solely on politics, teaching basic skills, dealing with feelings, or working to organize a community. However all of these different aspects of the work are necessary and have to be balanced in one's life. All of them must also be tempered by a central concern for one's students' lives. If skills or politics or feelings or curriculum or community meetings become more important than the children you work with, it is time to rethink your role, perhaps do something else and come back when you are fresh and can center your work on your students once more. There is no need to be afraid that your skills will not be necessary. There will always be places that need your help in their struggles. It will be years before our schools will be sane—as many years as it takes for this to become a sane society, for schools are just a small part of the problem in our society. As teachers the best we can do is use the skills we develop as part of the larger struggle to create a society based on collective responsibility rather than anxiety and personal greed.

APPENDIX:
RESEARCH DATA SUPPORTING
EDUCATIONAL CHANGE

MANY TIMES SCHOOL authorities will ask if there is any research to support educational change. For a while I have been relying on a few informal sources to document the need for change. However this is no longer necessary. Recently Wayne Jennings, director of the Saint Paul Open School in St. Paul, Minnesota and a Ph.D. from the University of Minnesota, as well as a magician and teacher of magic, and Joe Nathan, a teacher and trainer of change agents in education at the Saint Paul Open School, prepared a paper describing all the research supporting educational change. It is an invaluable weapon for teachers and for this reason I am reprinting their paper in full. Some of the results might astonish you as they did me.

STARTLING/DISTURBING RESEARCH

For over fifty years, studies have been conducted that document the effectiveness of educational programs operating much differently from 95 percent of the public schools in this country. This research leads us to question most practices in our schools.

Much of this research is not well known. Until the last several years, neither was the history of certain ethnic groups and women in our country. Just as history books must be revised to reflect more accurately the experiences of different groups, so must education histories be changed to include the startling, disturbing research that follows.

The studies are divided into two sections. The first describes results of experimental programs. The second presents research on the effects of traditional schools.

Experimental Practices

One of the most extraordinary experiments ever conducted in American education was the Eight-Year Study (Aikin, 1942). This study occurred during the 1930s. Thirty high schools signed an agreement with 300 colleges so that their graduates were freed from the usual college entrance requirements. This meant the high schools didn't have to use grades, class rank, required courses, credits, and so on. They could experiment with their curriculum and organization.

Some 1500 students from the experimental schools were paired with 1500 students from similar but nonexperimental schools and matched for sex, age, intelligence, family background, race, and other factors. The study found that students who came from experimental schools did as well or better at college in terms of grade point average, participation in extracurricular events, critical thinking, aesthetic judgment, knowledge of contemporary affairs, and so forth.

Further analysis of the data yields some startling results. When students who came from the six most experimental schools were compared with those from traditional schools, there were great differences in college attainment. Finally, the two most experimental schools (where practices were indeed unlike those in other schools—extensive learning in the community; volunteers brought in to work with students; advisor-advisee systems established; students teaching other students; interdisciplinary, problem-solving curriculum; and so forth) were selected. Graduates of these two schools were compared with traditional school graduates and the study found experimental school graduates were "strikingly more successful" (Aikin, p. 113).

The Eight-Year Study was one of the most significant and exciting studies of American education. Similar studies yielded essentially the same results.

One of the schools in the Eight-Year Study was the Ohio State University Lab School. The students who graduated in 1938 wrote a book called *Were We Guinea Pigs?* (Class of 1938). In general they liked their school but of course had little to compare it with since most had gone to the Lab School throughout their high school years. Many years later, a decision was made to follow up on the "guinea pigs" to see what happened to them in later life. The book *Guinea Pigs 20 Years Later* (Willis, 1961) came out in 1961. An extensive interview and a lengthy questionnaire were obtained from each graduate. These people were then between thirty-five and forty years old. The study found that the "guinea pigs" had been strikingly successful in life. Then they were compared with subjects in the

Terman study of genius who were about the same age, and the graduates of Princeton University where similar follow-up had been conducted, and who also were about the same age. In these comparisons, the experimental high school graduates came out ahead. They more often expressed satisfaction with life, were judged leaders in their various professions, had more stable family lives, possessed better self-accepting attitudes, and were mentioned more frequently in *Who's Who.*

Since 1970, a number of schools have been established which make use of curriculum and organization ideas developed by the experimental schools of the thirties or developed even earlier by John Dewey and other progressive educators.

Virtually every evaluation of these contemporary alternative schools shows students doing as well or better in the test scores than students in traditional schools, feeling much better about themselves and their ability to accomplish things for themselves, and having a much better attitude toward school and learning. These results come from alternative schools in Cambridge, Chicago, Hartford, Los Angeles, Minneapolis, Providence, Philadelphia, and St. Paul. (See references cited.)

One might wonder if alternative schools have atypical populations. The National Alternative Schools Program's *Survey of Public Alternative Schools* (1974, p. 5) studied 300 public alternative schools and found that their average student body was more diverse racially and economically than the country's population. Their study also reported an average of two applicants for every alternative school opening.

A number of schools specifically work with students who are rejects of traditional schools. Harlem Prep in New York City was established for dropouts of other schools; 95 percent of its graduates go on to college. Harlem Prep had one of the highest percentages in the country of graduates who also complete college.

The Career Study Center in St. Paul, Minn. takes only those students who are not experiencing success in the traditional high schools. In fact, high schools nominate candidates for this school. These students typically attend their old schools about 50 percent of the time. Seventy percent are in trouble with the law, and the schools and the parents are at their wits' end to build a proper program for them. After some time in the progressively designed program at CSC, attendance rises to 80 percent, they get out of trouble, and parents can't quite believe the change in attitude toward schooling. Ninety percent graduate, although the original prognosis was that only 10 percent would complete school. The Career Study Center was so successful that a second center has been established.

It's too early to have results from these programs similar to those of the

Eight-Year Study. However, other research indicates that the kind of success today's alternative schools report will result in more effective, competent, and stable adults. Recent studies challenge traditional notions of ways to predict success in later life.

For example, there is close to a national mania about graduation from high school. However, one study (Feldstein, 1974, p. 20) compared students enrolled in California colleges that accepted anyone who applied, irrespective of whether they had completed high school. Some 32,000 records were examined. Seven percent of these California college students didn't have a high school diploma. The grade point average for the non-high school graduates was 2.56 and for all students, 2.51. The data were then corrected for age, sex, marital status, veteran status, full-time versus part-time, and family income. In all cases, the non-high school graduates were doing as well as or better than the high school graduates.

Even more startling are a pair of studies that question the value of grades and test scores in predicting success. There are two major college entrance examination organizations in this country: the American College Testing Service (ACT) and the College Entrance Examination Boards (CEEB). The ACT recently completed a study (Munday and Davis, 1974) of itself that compared the value of four factors in predicting success (as measured by self-satisfaction and participation in a variety of community activities) two years after college. The factors were: (1) major achievement in what most high schools call "extracurricular activity" (debate, speech, journalism, and so forth); (2) high grades in high school; (3) high grades in college; (4) high scores on the ACT. Three of the four factors were found to be of no predictive value. The only factor that could be used to predict success in later life was achievement in "extracurricular activities."

In addition to the ACT study the Scholastic Aptitude Test (the core of the CEEB) was examined for its accuracy in predicting how successful a person might be at a chosen career upon graduation from college (Wallach, 1972). The results were that "the SAT's offered virtually no clue to capacity for significant intellectual or creative contributions in mature life" (Wallach, 1972). That is to say there was virtually no correlation between high scores on the SAT's and success in life. This study also found that the best predictor of creativity in mature life was a person's performance during youth in independent self-sustained ventures. Those youngsters who had many hobbies, interests, and jobs, or were active in extracurricular activities were more likely to be successful in later life. This study also found that deans of colleges are increasingly reliant on the SAT scores. In other words, the colleges are being badly misled about whom they are accepting on the basis of test scores. Both studies show test scores predict who will do well (in grades) at college, but that such academic success has *almost nothing* to do with success in later life.

There are many studies that found a nearly zero correlation between college grades and later success in such fields as medicine, law, education, engineering.

Project Talent interviewed 1000 thirty-year-olds in the United States in 1975, in what is believed to be one of the most nationally representative follow-up studies. Dr. Robert Gagne, one of the ten reviewing educators, summarized the findings in one terse sentence: "The evidence of these interviews suggests that high school education as a whole serves no very useful purpose" (Project Talent, 1976, p. 2).

There is ample evidence that organizing total schools in very different ways makes sense. Earlier reports were mentioned from alternative schools indicating strong success. Most of the alternative schools are total programs. It's also important to look at results of studies that deal only with parts of a program.

A study on math is especially interesting. Ordinarily, the beginning age for teaching math is six. In an international study, researchers found some places where math was delayed until age seven, and in a few rare instances, age eight. The study found that students who were taught math last caught up with those who were taught earlier. Extremes of as much as two years of instruction made no difference in math achievement. In addition, those who had had the latest initial math instruction had fewer negative attitudes toward school and themselves (Husen, 1967).

In the area of remedial reading a number of studies indicate a substantial gain in reading achievement after remedial reading instruction. Within a year these gains disappear and the child appears to have made only the progress one would have expected without the remedial instruction (Silberberg, 1969, p. 217).

It has been known for a very long time that achievement on standardized tests is a very stable score and not very amenable to change. Considerable reductions in time spent on reading, math, and spelling (the basics!) did not reduce achievement scores according to a 1932 review of studies (Beatley, 1932). This result has been affirmed many times since.

The Plowden Report in England found that the integrated day approach was becoming increasingly prevalent in English primary schools. Students who did not have the usual long, thorough, carefully graded and sequenced reading, math, and writing instruction did as well as those students who did have this emphasis on lesson-hearing and workbooks (Central Advisory Council, 1967). That stunning finding led to much interest in the open classroom in the United States.

Numerous studies indicate that children can be very effective at teaching other students. Usually the studies show that the student being taught, usually younger, learns better than would be expected, and that the older student or tutor learns a good deal more even when he or she was weak in the subject. Teaching what one has learned to another appears to be a very effective learning reinforcement (Gartner, Kohler, Riessman, 1971).

There is a growing acceptance of different organizations for learning. Public alternative schools have increased from fewer than ten in 1970 to over 1200 (Barr, 1974, p. 5). Parents and students who have participated in these programs often are their best advocates. The research done on alternative schools indicates that hopes have been fulfilled. At least one regional accreditation association, North Central Association, has developed new standards so that alternative schools could be evaluated and accredited. Last year three alternative schools in the Midwest received accreditation under these standards. Thus, those pushing for new kinds of learning have strong support for their position. The next section will look at questions raised by research about practices of most schools in this country.

Traditional Schools/Learning

Many commonly held beliefs about the effectiveness of our schools are questionable. Among these are beliefs that children need to be in school five days per week, that increased expenditures to do the same thing will make a significant difference, that schools prepare students well for our society, and that the environment of most schools is conducive to learning.

Two little-known studies pose major questions about the necessity of so much formal school time. The Unity Maine School District found itself in financial trouble four years ago and decided to have a four-day week for students to save money on busing and cafeteria costs. The staff continued with a five-day week, with one day devoted to in-service training and retraining. The Maine Department of Education was upset over this and gave its approval for the plan only with the stipulation that extensive tests be given to compare student achievement with previous years. These tests were conducted by the University of Maine. The evaluation director's conclusion was that the four-day student week, "Gains clearly outweighed losses when considering the grade equivalent scores of all students tested" (Drummond, 1972). The Maine Commissioner of Education congratulated the district on its "foresight and initiative."

Similar striking scores came about after the Philadelphia teacher's strike in 1972–1973. The strike lasted eight weeks, with some schools closed and others open the entire time. At the end of the year students who attended full-time during the strike were compared with those who were out the entire eight weeks. No significant differences in achievement were found between the two groups.

A series of investigations on student attitudes found that by late elementary school age nearly 20 percent of children are identified as against school and that the remaining majority "do not feel strongly about their classroom experience one way or another" (Jackson, 1968, p. 60). One study found that even children classified as satisfied with their school experience describe it with such adjectives as "boring, uncertain, dull, restless, and inadequate" (Jackson, 1968).

Such results lead to questions about what is happening in traditional schools "behind the classroom door." A study that used that phrase as its title listed well-known principles of- learning. Researchers went into the schools to see to what extent these principles of learning were in practice. They saw very few instances in classrooms (Goodlad, 1970). This study's finding is similar to others in which teachers have been questioned about their knowledge of modern principles of learning, i.e., students should be actively involved in their own learning, students can learn from a variety of people, success leads to future success, and so forth. In each case, teachers know very little about such principles, or when they do verbalize the principles, their learning principles are seldom seen in application in their classroom.

Given such recognition by teachers, it's not too surprising that those entering the average U.S. classroom find a good deal of boring activity and a sense of program dullness. In such a study, researchers found that in the course of one school year attitudes toward most school subjects become measurably more negative (Neale, Gill, and Tismer, 1970) and that, with each advancing year in school, children's evaluations of teachers and curriculum as well as of themselves as people become increasingly less favorable (Neale and Proshek, 1967, Yamamoto, Thomas, and Karnes, 1969).

This finding is similar to mental health studies that indicate that about one-third of the adults are seriously ill, about one-third need some attention, and about one-third have good mental health (Hollingshead and Redlich, 1958). Not too happy a record for our society, or for the schools that are supposed to help people achieve their potential.

Americans clearly are capable of knowing and doing much more than they are doing at present. A recent United States Office of Education study asked 7,500 adults questions to see if they were competent at tasks the researchers felt were vital for survival in the society (Northcutt, 1975). The tasks included knowing where to apply for social security benefits; how to figure which was a better bargain, ½-gallon of milk for 79¢ or a gallon for $1.10; how to read a sample ballot; and so forth. The study found that from 20 to 33 percent of the adults couldn't achieve minimum levels, depending on the tasks, and that another 20 to 30 percent of the adults functioned but without proficiency!

Studies of high school-age youths indicate that rather high numbers have seriously undemocratic views and tend to reject typical American ideals of liberty and opportunity for all (Remmers, 1957).

This seems related to the experiences of people who have taken the Bill of Rights from door to door, disguised as a petition to be signed. They found few takers, with some people commenting that it looked like a communist document. This shouldn't be surprising if we look carefully at the systematic denial of democratic decision making that characterizes virtually every public school in this country.

Many expensive efforts have been made to accept the basic operating methods of most schools, changing a few techniques. John Henry Martin became superintendent of an affluent suburb near New York City. He convinced the school board to increase the budget by 35 percent in order to make many school improvements. Class size was reduced, various specialists were hired, training programs were started for staff, new materials were purchased, and so on. Some sixty improvements were made, but the basic organization and curriculum methods of traditional schools were retained. After a couple of years, psychometricians were hired to see what difference had occurred as a result of these expenditures. There was no difference (Martin, 1972). One modification was to bring in remedial teachers to help those who don't seem to learn to read in the early grades, though instruction was provided. Studies of remedial reading indicate immediate gains during the year instruction occurs, but regression to expected progress without remedial instruction one year later.

It is hard to understand why schools go on making such an extraordinary attempt to develop all students into excellent readers. That effort would be much better spent if it were to make students into good learners, for there are many ways to learn. Unfortunately schools base much of their effort on literary and academic achievement. Reading is a talent or aptitude distributed on a normal curve, similar to music and art, with the beginning age for reading from three to fourteen.

In an extraordinarily valuable article, Neil Postman points out the highly political nature of reading instruction in this country (Postman, 1970). Fortunes have and are being made by those who produce massive doses of reading curriculum material. In fact, the reading instruction/ materials industry is the single largest subindustry in education! Learning to read is not nearly as difficult as it has been made out to be in this country. Cynthia Brown has documented that Paulo Freire helped Brazilian adults learn to read in thirty hours or less, with extraordinarily simple, low-cost materials (Brown, 1975).

Freire's work suggests that the act of learning to read can be accomplished with a few hours of actual teaching. The acts of learning addition, subtraction, and other basic arithmetic functions may require only a few hours if we work with children when they are interested in learning, have the capacity, and have a background of concrete experiences that make that learning a simple, final conceptualization of some earlier intuitive learnings. William Rohwer says that the timing on instruction is probably inappropriate for 40 to 50 percent of the students (Rohwer, 1971). This seems conservative. He suggests that the prime time for most formal kinds of learning might be adolescence. The informal learning, interaction with materials, experimentation, observation, trial and error, and interaction with older and younger people will provide an enormously potent background of intuitive learnings when formal instruction begins.

All these studies raise fundamental questions about the relationship between what is known about learning and what schools are doing. Perhaps we should go back to consider the kind of learning that occurs before the age of five. By the time an average American child enters kindergarten, she or he has learned two of the most complex series of tasks to be confronted during a lifetime: to walk and to talk. The child has learned without lesson plans, grades, extensive curriculum materials, and certified teachers. In fact, if these things had been used, the above-mentioned research indicates there would have been serious learning problems! Instead, the child has role models of different ages, receives encouragement, and has people around who really care about the child. The child learns!

Two enormous studies suggest that schools might follow up on the model of being warm and friendly places. Coleman's study examined 600,000 students in the United States in an effort to test out what factors made a difference in achievement. Only two factors were found. They weren't class size, teacher preparation, per-pupil expenditures, or any of the usual factors that one would suspect. Instead, they were the child's sense of control over her or his own fate or destiny or sense of self-worth, and the kind of socioeconomic background the child came from (Coleman, 1967).

A second study duplicated the Coleman work by examining 258,000 students in 9,700 schools in twenty countries and came up with essentially the same findings (Platt, 1974). Obviously schools cannot control their students' background. However, they clearly can help the child develop a much better sense of control over her or his life, at least during the hours of 8:30 to 3:00. Clearly schools can do a much better job of helping students experience success.

Some people argue that schools which help all students experience success would be seriously out of touch with society, for our society requires intense competition in which not all can be winners. However, schools are established only to help students fit into every aspect of our society, no matter how inhumane. Isn't it possible that if more people felt better about themselves, the society would be more livable?

There are other ways that our schools already are out of touch with this society.

Many studies have criticized schools for being seriously out of phase with the rest of society. James Coleman believes that at the turn of the century, schools performed a valuable function of information sharing/dispensing. At that time, our society was "information poor and responsibility rich." The mass media did not exist, newspapers were scarce or came out weekly. Few people subscribed to them or to magazines. On the other hand, children of that era had many important responsibilities in the home, family business, or on the farm as workers and could see the direct relationship of their efforts to the well-being of the family (Coleman, 1972).

Coleman sees the 1970s as a reversal from eighty years ago, so that schools are "responsibility poor and information rich," for children. However, Coleman says the schools act as though society were the same, that is, information poor and responsibility rich. The schools should reexamine their character he argues, and provide diverse experiences with opportunities for youths to learn how to handle responsibility. Schools should not worry so much about the information-giving since information will flow to students through many sources.

These recommendations are consistent with those of five major studies completed by national groups between 1972 and 1975, which provide sweeping suggestions for change in our schools. While each of these studies was conducted independent of the other, there is a remarkable similarity in their final recommendations. In general, these studies concluded that schools are inflexible (students who know a subject still have to take a course in it); most activities in school are done in lock-step, group-paced fashion; the products of high school are not very competent as citizens, consumers, parents, and workers, and seem poorly informed about the current world while possessing troubling undemocratic attitudes (Panel on Youth, 1973; Reform of Secondary Education, 1973; Carnegie Commission, 1973; NASSP, 1972; RISE, 1975).

The five studies have many recommendations. They suggest what has come to be known as "Action Learning." This means students will be engaged in projects involving a payoff in terms of better life in the school or society. The studies recommend that students be much more involved in the community businesses, internships, work, and social service experiences. A second recommendation is that schools should operate on an extended day and year basis and that learning should increasingly be seen as a lifelong process. The studies recommend competency-based graduation so that students have to show they can perform specific acts related to life skills, and not be required to take courses covering skills they already have. A fourth recommendation is that secondary school be combined with college or vocational programs. Finally, these studies insist that students and parents should have a variety of programs from which to choose, or alternatives.

We have come full circle. Over the past seventy years, critics of American schools have often differed. Some have chosen to establish different kinds of programs. The heirs of these reformers in the 1970s are people who are developing alternative programs with expectations, curriculum, and opportunities very different from those in the traditional schools.

Those pushing for change in public schools have had remarkably little help from educational scholars in the universities. Most of the startling research mentioned in this article is never discussed or even cited in college and university classes. Taylor studied a representative cross section of college and universities where teachers are educated and concluded that the typical teacher education graduate is expected to "learn what he is taught from texts which raise few fundamental questions by teachers who are older versions of himself and of what he will some day be" (Taylor, 1969, p. 20). Taylor also found that college educational experiences typically encourage teachers to continue to function within the simple concept of curriculum, consisting of a prescribed pattern of courses distributed among various subjects supposedly covering specific topics that are prerequisite for courses to follow (Taylor, 1969).

With relatively few major exceptions, college people offer very little help to those trying to make fundamental changes and improvements in our learning system. Indeed, educational scholars often frustrate changes within their own institutions as well as in schools.

Yet change must come! The research in this article suggests that we should not be upset by experiments in education but should welcome them. We should support program and curriculum experimentation. We should not be afraid to be open to ideas and to try some things ourselves.

It may be that current practices are the worst possible way we could have arranged for the education of the young. Research findings suggest that test scores on standardized achievement tests are not likely to drop in school experiments. These findings suggest that the state of educational research is primitive and that our schools may more resemble factories turning out identical products than programs trying to help individuals reach their unique potential.

Educators should view the curriculum not only as those experiences which the schools control for youth but also as all the life experiences irrespective of time and place. Learning is a lifelong process best performed when self-directed.

Change is difficult to understand. People who visit experimental programs or alternative programs obviously are prisoners of their past experiences. They often find the visit to experimental or alternative schools a mind-boggling experience, and can't imagine that the results would be improved people or more responsible citizens. The conventional thinking in many regular schools is that experimental schools are places of great permissiveness and therefore of sexual license, little learning, rude behavior, and so forth. This does not coincide with the facts but makes for interesting gossip.

What these attitudes suggest is that most educators are not serious students of learning and may be unable to recognize when or how it occurs. Instead they go on with the same teach, recite, lesson-hearing, test, dry-as-dust modes that they themselves find boring.

Alternative school staffs and parents sometimes become disheartened or discouraged. Often they expect all problems to be solved by establishing a new structure or organization. It's vital that people not confuse the value of the ideas and techniques they're using with difficulties they have in actually carrying them off. Working with young people is hard work, and we always know more than we're able to do at any particular moment. Still, most surviving experimental or alternative schools find their programs get better and better, and the student/parent satisfaction increases steadily.

Change is justified. It's justified because there are problems in public schools, because research says experimentation has good results, can be done quickly, and will be accepted if parents and students are given choices.

The real barriers to educational change exist in leadership positions in American education, and these are primarily states of mind. Many people have been able to get exemptions from the state regulations, or interpret new practices to fit the state regulations, or simply confront the regulations as being obsolete.

Changes can be made in public schools. There are models, customers, and support. It can be made. Those who want public schools to survive but refuse to help make major changes should think about the dinosaurs' experience. The dinosaurs didn't change to meet new requirements and became extinct!

References Cited

Aikin, Wilford. *Story of the Eight Year Study.* New York: Harper & Brothers, 1942.

Barr, Robert. "Growth of Public Alternative Schools," *Changing Schools,* no. 12, 1975, p. 3.

Bauer, David. "What Research Says about Interest in Learning," *Educational Leadership,* November, 1975, pp. 100–104.

Beatley, Bancroft. *Achievement in Junior High School.* Cambridge, Mass.: Harvard University Press, 1932.

Brown, Cynthia. *Literacy in 30 Hours.* London: Expression Printers, 1975. Available from Center for Open Learning and Teaching, Berkeley, California.

California Commission for Reform of Intermediate and Secondary Education. *RISE Report.* Sacramento: California State Department of Education, 1975.

Cambridge Alternative Public School. *Evaluation Materials.* Available from Leonard Solo, Principal, Cambridge Alternative Public School, 54 Essex St., Cambridge, Mass.

Carnegie Commission on Higher Education. *Continuity and Discontinuity.* New York: McGraw-Hill, 1973.

Central Advisory Council for Education (England). *Children and Their Primary Schools,* 2 volumes. London: Her Majesty's Stationery Office, 1967. (Often called the Plowden Report.)

Class of 1938, Ohio State University Lab School. *Were We Guinea Pigs?* New York: Henry Holt, 1938.

Coleman, James. "The Children Have Outgrown the Schools," *Psychology Today,* February 1972, pp. 72–76.

Coleman, James, et. al. *Equality of Educational Opportunity.* Washington, D.C.: Superintendent of Documents, 1967.

Drummond, Robert. Preliminary Report–Research & Evaluation Team, University of Maine. Orono, Me.: Achievement Testing Program for MSAD #3, mimeographed, 1972.

Evaluation of Alternative Learning Project. Providence: Providence Public Schools, 1972; 1973; 1974.

Evaluations of Marcy Open School and Southeast Free School. Minneapolis: Southeast Alternative Project, 1973; 1974; 1975.

Evaluations of St. Paul Open School. St. Paul: St. Paul Public Schools, 1972; 1973; 1974.

Feldstein, Donald. "Who Needs High School?" *Social Policy,* May/June 1974, p. 20.

Gartner, Alan, Kohler, Mary, and Riessman, Frank. *Children Teach Children.* New York: Harper & Row, 1971.

Goodlad, John. *Behind the Classroom Door.* Belmont, Cal.: Wadsworth, 1970.

Hollingshead, R. and Redlich, F. *Social Class and Mental Health.* New York: Wiley, 1958.

Hoyt, D. P. *Relationship between College Grades and Adult Achievement: A Review of the Literature,* ACT Research Report #7. Iowa City: ACT Program, 1965.

Husen, T. *International Study of Achievement in Mathematics,* vol. 2. Uppsala, Sweden: Almquist & Wilsells, 1967.

Jackson, P. W. *Life in Classrooms.* New York: Holt, Rinehart & Winston, 1968.

Los Angeles School District Research and Evaluation Branch. *Four Alternative Schools, 1974–1975,* Report #345. Los Angeles: Los Angeles Schools, 1975.

Martin, John Henry. "Chairman's Digest," U.S. Department of Health, Education and Welfare, Office of Education, Panel on High Schools and Adolescent Education, mimeographed, April 1974.

Martin, John Henry and Harrison, Charles. *Free to Learn.* Englewood Cliffs, N.J.: Prentice-Hall, 1972.

Munday, L. A. and David, J. C. *Varieties of Accomplishment after College: Perspectives on the Meaning of Academic Talent,* ACT Research Report #62. Iowa City: ACT Program, 1974.

National Alternative Schools Program. *Survey of Public Alternative Schools,* Amherst, Mass.: National Alternative Schools Program, mimeographed, 1974.

National Association of Secondary School Principals. *American Youth in the Mid-Seventies.* Reston, Va.: NASSP, 1972.

National Commission on the Reform of Secondary Education. *Reform of Secondary Education.* New York: McGraw-Hill, 1973.

Neale, D. C., and Proshek, J. M. "School Related Attitudes of Culturally Disadvantaged Elementary School Children," *Journal of Educational Psychology* 58, 1967, pp. 238–44.

Neale, D. C., Gill, N., and Tismer, W. "Relationship Between Attitudes Toward School Subjects and School Achievement," *Journal of Educational Research* 63 (1970), pp. 232–37.

Northcutt, Norvell. *Adult Functional Competency: A Summary.* Washington, D.C.: U.S. Department of Health, Education and Welfare, 1975.

Panel on Youth of the President's Science Advisory Committee. *Youth: Transition to Adulthood.* Washington, D.C.: Superintendent of Document, 1973.

Platt, William. "Policy Making and International Studies in Educational Evaluations," *Phi Delta Kappan,* March 1974, p. 451.

Postman, Neil. "The Politics of Reading," *Harvard Educational Review* 40, no. 2 (May 1970).

Project Talent, reported in *The School Administrator* 33, no. 2 (February 1976), p. 2.

Remmers, H. H. and Radler, D. H. *American Teenager.* Indianapolis: Bobbs-Merrill, 1957.

Rohwer, William. "Prime Time for Education: Early Childhood or Adolescence?" *Harvard Educational Review* 41, no. 3 (August 1971).

Silberburg, Margaret, and Silberberg, Norman. "Myths in Remedial Education," *Journal of Learning Disabilities* 2, no. 4 (April 1969), pp. 209–17.

Taylor, H. *The World as Teacher.* Garden City, N.Y.: Doubleday, 1969.

Tenenbaum, L. "Uncontrolled Expression of Children's Attitudes Toward School," *Elementary School Journal* 40, pp. 670–78.

Wallace, Michael. "Psychology of Talent and Graduate Education." Paper Presented at International Conference on Cognitive Styles and Creativity in Higher Education, sponsored by the Graduate Record Examinations Board, Montreal, November 1972.

Willis, Margaret. *Guinea Pigs After 20 Years.* Columbus: Ohio State University Press, 1961.

Yamamoto, K., Thomas, E. C., and Karner, E. A. "School-Related Attitudes in Middle-School Age Students," *American Educational Research Journal* 6 (1969), pp. 191–206.

INDEX